Cambridge Elements ≡

Elements in Religion and Violence
edited by
James R. Lewis
University of Tromsø
Margo Kitts
Hawai'i Pacific University

ISLAM AND SUICIDE ATTACKS

Pieter Nanninga
University of Groningen

CAMBRIDGE
UNIVERSITY PRESS

CAMBRIDGE
UNIVERSITY PRESS

University Printing House, Cambridge CB2 8BS, United Kingdom

One Liberty Plaza, 20th Floor, New York, NY 10006, USA

477 Williamstown Road, Port Melbourne, VIC 3207, Australia

314–321, 3rd Floor, Plot 3, Splendor Forum, Jasola District Centre,
New Delhi – 110025, India

79 Anson Road, #06–04/06, Singapore 079906

Cambridge University Press is part of the University of Cambridge.

It furthers the University's mission by disseminating knowledge in the pursuit of
education, learning, and research at the highest international levels of excellence.

www.cambridge.org
Information on this title: www.cambridge.org/9781108712651
DOI: 10.1017/9781108670524

© Pieter Nanninga 2019

First published 2019

A catalogue record for this publication is available from the British Library.

ISBN 978-1-108-71265-1 Paperback
ISSN 2397-9496 (online)
ISSN 2514-3786 (print)

Islam and Suicide Attacks

Elements in Religion and Violence

DOI: 10.1017/9781108670524
First published online: October 2019

Pieter Nanninga

University of Groningen
Author for correspondence: p.g.t.nanninga@rug.nl

ABSTRACT: This Element explores the disputed relationship between Islam and suicide attacks. Drawing from primary source material as well as existing scholarship from fields such as terrorism studies and religious studies, it argues that Islam as a generic category is not an explanatory factor in suicide attacks. Rather, it claims that we need to study how organisations and individuals in their particular contexts draw tools such as Islamic martyrdom traditions, ritual practices and perceptions on honour and purity from their cultural repertoire to shape, justify and give meaning to the bloodshed.

KEYWORDS: Islam, jihadism, martyrdom, religious studies, suicide attacks, terrorism studies

ISBNs: 9781108712651 (PB), 9781108670524 (OC)
ISSNs: 2397-9496 (online), ISSN 2514-3786 (print)

Contents

Introduction

From Hezbollah's bombings in the early 1980s to present-day attacks by al-Qaeda and the Islamic State, suicide attacks seem to be a predominantly Islamic phenomenon. Over two-thirds of the approximately 6,600 suicide attacks between 1981 and 2017 were committed by jihadist groups in just four Muslim-majority countries: Syria, Iraq, Afghanistan and Pakistan (START 2018; CPOST 2018). Since that period, the Islamic State alone has carried out more than one thousand suicide attacks in Iraq and Syria in defence of its self-proclaimed caliphate (Winter 2017). Suicide attacks by Islamic groups and organisations have become an almost daily occurrence in recent years. Moreover, the organisers and perpetrators of these attacks typically emphasise the Islamic nature of their operations. These men 'destroy themselves to make God's word supreme', Osama bin Laden claimed of al-Qaeda's suicide bombers (al-Sahab 2007a), while the Islamic State celebrates its attackers as men who are 'in love with this religion' and 'guided by the light that leads their way' towards the lands of eternity (Wilayat Ninawa 2017).[1]

This raises questions about the relationship between Islam and suicide attacks. Why have organisations in the Muslim world in particular embraced this mode of attack since the early 1980s? Why have thousands of individuals killed themselves amidst their enemies in the name of Islam? What is the role of Islamic traditions about martyrdom and self-sacrificial violence?

In public discourse, opinions about the role of Islam in suicide attacks have often been straightforward, either blaming Islam as a causal factor or exonerating Islam as an essentially peaceful religion that is being profaned

---

[1] Due to the sensitive nature of the primary sources referred to in this Element, some of the files will be removed from the websites listed in the bibliography. The bibliography provides references to English subtitled or translated versions of the Arabic-language sources (if available). The author has adapted these translations for reasons of style and accuracy, so quotations in this Element regularly deviate from the translations offered in the referenced sources. The sources have all been downloaded by the author and can be accessed upon written request (p.g.t. nanninga@rug.nl).

by terrorists. In scholarly literature, opinions have been more nuanced. Yet academics, too, have disagreed. In the case of al-Qaeda (see Nanninga 2017), for example, Robert A. Pape considers the role of religion only to be secondary in explaining the group's suicide attacks. 'For al-Qaeda, religion matters', he claims, 'but mainly in the context of national resistance to foreign occupation' (Pape 2006: 104). Assaf Moghadam fundamentally disagrees, however, emphasising that al-Qaeda's long-term mission is 'fundamentally religious', as it aims 'to wage a cosmic struggle against an unholy alliance of Christians and Jews' (Moghadam 2006a: 718). Others have proposed variations on these arguments, for instance by distinguishing between al-Qaeda's 'almost purely political' immediate objectives and its 'distinctly Islamic' ultimate aims (Sedgwick 2004).

This Element further explores the disputed relationship between Islam and suicide attacks. By drawing from scholarship as well as primary source material, it argues that Islam as a generic category is not an explanatory factor. Rather, just like other religious traditions, Islam provides a rich repertoire of historical narratives, beliefs, values, attitudes and practices that lend themselves to multiple interpretations and uses – both peaceful and violent. Muslims, including organisers, perpetrators and supporters of suicide attacks, selectively draw from this repertoire to shape and give meaning to their lives and the world around them. This Element therefore argues that to understand the role of Islam in suicide attacks, we should acknowledge the agency of the actors involved. Rather than focusing on the role of Islam per se, we should ask how, why and under which concrete historical, political, social and cultural circumstances they select and assemble particular 'tools' from their inherited tradition to shape, justify and give meaning to their contested practices. Only then can we begin to understand the complex relationship between the Islamic tradition and the thousands of men and women who believed that sacrificing themselves for their cause was the right thing to do.

After introducing the topic of suicide attacks with a discussion of the relevant terminology and the history of the phenomenon, Section 1 will provide an overview of the most prominent explanations from the field of terrorism studies on both the organisational and individual levels. Section 2 will subsequently focus on the role of religion in suicide attacks. Based on insights from the field of religious studies and related fields and disciplines, it will identify several challenges to current approaches to the topic and offer some suggestions for developing a more nuanced approach. These insights will be illustrated in Section 3 by examining a number of themes that are often associated with suicide attacks, such as early Islamic martyrdom traditions, perceptions on honour and purity, and ritualisation.

1 Suicide Attacks

Since the 9/11 attacks in New York and Washington, there has been a marked increase in the scholarly study of suicide attacks. This section introduces the main insights from these studies. After providing the necessary background by briefly discussing the relevant terminology and the history of suicide attacks, it will discuss current explanations of the phenomenon. The section will mainly focus on the Muslim world, after which the role of religion, and Islam in particular, will be explicitly examined in Sections 2 and 3.

1.1 Defining Suicide Attacks

Despite the increased prominence of suicide attacks in the twenty-first century, the term 'suicide attacks' and its meanings have remained ambiguous. First of all, it is important to acknowledge that suicide attacks are not a single unified method of violence (Crenshaw 2007: 162). The means as well as the targets of suicide attacks have varied widely since the early 1980s. Moreover, suicide attacks have often been used alongside other forms of violence, such as shooting sprees and hostage-taking. Hence, as Martha Crenshaw (2001) has rightly noted, suicide attacks are not a sui generis phenomenon, but should rather be conceived as part of the repertoire of action that is available to organisations and individuals.

The question of what exactly constitutes a 'suicide attack' is also contested (Moghadam 2006b; Crenshaw 2007: 135–40). Suicide attacks are traditionally defined as attacks in which self-aware individuals purposely cause their own deaths by killing themselves along with their chosen targets (Moghadam 2006b: 18). Many authors further refine this definition by claiming that suicide attacks are attacks in which success is dependent upon the death of the perpetrator (Schweitzer 2000: 78; Moghadam 2006b: 18–19). This so-called narrow definition thus excludes high-risk operations in which the perpetrator is prepared to die and might even anticipate death but has a chance of surviving. Other scholars, however, argue that the perpetrator's *intent* to die is crucial and therefore adopt a broader definition that includes high-risk operations (Winter 2017: 4). These debates are important not only for collecting comparable data (Moghadam 2006b: 19–20), but also because they illustrate the ambiguity of the phenomenon under study in this Element.

In addition to the precise definition of the term 'suicide attacks', the term itself is controversial. Many authors have preferred alternatives, the most widespread of which is probably 'suicide terrorism'. In line with Crenshaw's observations above, this term emphasises that suicide attacks are a subset of terrorism. The term 'terrorism' itself is contested, however, not only because of the lack of an accepted definition (Hoffman 2017: 1–44), but also because it is considered as more biased than alternatives such as 'suicide attacks', 'suicide missions' and 'suicide operations'. Moreover, most definitions of 'terrorism' only include acts of violence against non-military targets. If employed strictly, the term therefore excludes the hundreds of suicide attacks executed against armed forces in countries such as Afghanistan, Iraq and Israel.

Finally, the terms mentioned above are contested for an additional reason: their association with suicide. As will be further discussed in Section 1.3, research has convincingly demonstrated that suicide bombers cannot be compared to ordinary suicides who kill themselves in order to escape life (Moghadam 2008: 27). Moreover, the association with suicide is strongly resisted by the perpetrators themselves and their supporters. In the Muslim world, suicide (*intihar*) is highly controversial, also because several passages in the Qur'an and *hadith* (allegedly) reject the practice.[2] Muslim scholars have repeatedly invoked these traditions to renounce suicide attacks as un-Islamic. The perpetrators of suicide attacks and their supporters, however, argue that these operations should not be considered as acts

---

[2] Although the Qur'an is not completely unambiguous, texts such as Q. 4:29 are interpreted as forbidding suicide. Moreover, according to several *hadith*s, the Prophet strongly condemned suicide (Rosenthal 2010).

of suicide. Rather, they typically refer to the concept of martyrdom (*istish-had*) to frame and give meaning to their actions (Hafez 2006a: 55). Accordingly, suicide attacks are often labelled as 'martyrdom-seeking operations' (*'amaliyyat istishhadiyya*) and their perpetrators as 'martyrs' (*shudada'*, sing. *shahid*) or 'martyrdom seekers' (*istishhadiyyun*). The insiders' labels thus have rather different connotations to the term 'suicide', as will be further discussed when focusing on the notion of martyrdom in Section 3.1. While I, for the purpose of this study, will stick to the term 'suicide attack', it is crucial to take this point into account when trying to understand why people kill themselves alongside their enemies.

1.2 Suicide Attacks: A Short History

The definition of 'suicide attack' one prefers also has consequences for discussing the history of the phenomenon. When adopting a broad definition of the term, one could include cases such as the biblical figure of Samson, who reportedly killed himself along with his Philistine enemies by pushing apart the central pillars of the temple in which he was set for their entertainment (Judges 16). Another case often referred to by scholars studying suicide attacks is the medieval sect of the Ismaili Assassins (*hashashin*), whose preferred tactic was to assassinate leaders of their Sunni and Christian opponents by means of a dagger. According to Bernard Lewis (2003), the Assassins were almost always caught and killed afterwards, usually not even attempting to escape.

Yet, whereas self-sacrificial violence is found in all periods of human history, suicide attacks according to the narrow definition are dependent on modern technologies and are therefore a modern phenomenon. One of the first evident cases of suicide bombings is provided by Russian anarchists in the late nineteenth and early twentieth century, several of whom killed themselves alongside their opponents by exploding dynamite. A more prominent case, albeit of a different nature and not falling under most definitions of (suicide) 'terrorism' because it concerned members of regular armed forces, is that of the Japanese kamikaze pilots, who carried out thousands of suicide missions during the final phase of World War II (Hill 2005).

Nevertheless, most scholars studying the phenomenon are interested in explaining the contemporary wave of suicide attacks, and therefore start their historical overviews in the early 1980s. Based on insights from these studies, we could roughly distinguish between two (overlapping) phases, the first of which was dominated by nationally oriented resistance groups adopting the method of suicide attacks from the early 1980s and the second by the so-called globalisation of the phenomenon that was instigated by al-Qaeda in the late 1990s and early 2000s (Khosrokhavar 2005; Schweitzer 2006; Moghadam 2008).

First Phase: Local Conflicts

The first phase started on 15 December 1981, when a member of the Shia group al-Da'wa directed a car rigged with explosives into the Iraqi Embassy in Beirut. Suicide attacks against Israeli Defence Forces as well as Western targets in Lebanon soon followed, the most devastating of which were those against the US Embassy, US military barracks and a French compound in Beirut in 1983, which killed over 350 people in total. That it was Shia groups pioneering the tactic during the Lebanese Civil War comes as no surprise given their links to the recently born Islamic Republic of Iran. In the context of the Iranian revolution of 1979 and Iran-Iraq War that soon followed, martyrdom increasingly became an objective to be actively pursued by believers (see Section 3.1). This idea was adopted by prominent Lebanese clerics such as Musa al-Sadr and Muhammad Husayn Fadlallah and put into practice by Iranian-backed groups in the country. Soon to gain predominance among these groups was Hezbollah, to which the 1983 Beirut bombings would eventually also be attributed (Norton 2007). The results of these bombings in particular were significant for the further history of the phenomenon. Soon after these attacks, the USA and France decided to withdraw their troops from Lebanon. As a result, suicide attacks were considered a successful tactic from the outset (Pape 2006: 129–39; Pedahzur 2005: 45–54; Moghadam 2008: 17–22).

It was the (perceived) success of the tactic rather than its ideological legitimations that contributed to its spread, as is illustrated by the fact that secular groups in Lebanon also adopted it. Moreover, non-Muslim groups elsewhere also appropriated the tactic. In the late 1980s, the Liberation

Tigers of Tamil Eelam (LTTE) started using suicide attacks in their struggle against the Sri Lankan army. Drawing from Hindu traditions of self-sacrifice, the LTTE carried out more than 140 suicide attacks between 1987 and 2001, becoming infamous for the introduction of the suicide belt that was used to assassinate high-profile opponents. The Kurdish Workers Party (PKK) embraced suicide attacks in its conflict with the Turkish state in 1996 and, some years later, Chechen rebels followed the same path against Russian armed forces during the Second Chechen War. In both cases, the majority of the bombers were women (Pape 2006: 208).

More eye-catching has been the case of the Palestinian suicide bombers, not least because the majority of them targeted civilians. Here, the tactic was pioneered by Hamas and the Palestinian Islamic Jihad in the wake of the Oslo I Accord in 1993, only to become widely used during the al-Aqsa Intifada that started in September 2000. During this uprising, Palestinians widely supported suicide attacks against Israel[3] and the spread of the practice was accompanied by a cult surrounding the martyrs (Oliver and Steinberg 2005). As a result, Fatah's al-Aqsa Martyrs Brigades and the Marxist Popular Front for the Liberation of Palestine (PFLP) also resorted to suicide attacks when their popularity started to decline (Hafez 2006b).

Second Phase: The Globalisation of Suicide Attacks

The above cases demonstrate that until the late 1990s suicide attacks had been predominantly used by religious and ethnonationalist groups engaged in local, asymmetrical conflicts evolving around independence and territorial claims. The late 1990s witnessed the rise of a new pattern of suicide attacks, however, which has been labelled the 'globalisation of martyrdom' (Moghadam 2008). This pattern has been characterised by an exceptional rise in the number of suicide attacks, as well as by their spread across the world. It was instigated by al-Qaeda and has been dominated by global jihadists.

Al-Qaeda adopted suicide attacks soon after it publicly announced its *jihad* against 'the Americans occupying the Land of the Two Holy Places'

---

[3] According to polls conducted by the Jerusalem Media and Communication Center around 70 per cent of Palestinians supported suicide attacks against Israel in 2011 and early 2012 (JMCC 2002).

(i.e. Saudi Arabia) in its 1996 'Declaration of War' (Bin Laden 1996). Inspired by the alleged successes of its Lebanese and Palestinian predecessors, as well as by its members of the Egyptian Islamic Jihad who had experimented with the tactic in the mid-1990s (Gerges 2005: 141–3), al-Qaeda's leaders became convinced of the tactical advantages of the method. 'Martyrdom operations', al-Zawahiri wrote in 2001, are 'the most successful way of inflicting damage against the opponent and the least costly to the mujahidin in terms of casualties'. Moreover, he suggested, they have the capacity to instil fear in the enemy and communicate messages to the audience, referring to violence as a 'language' (*lugha*) that is understood by the West (al-Zawahiri 2001: 243).

Accordingly, al-Qaeda learned from its predecessors, but meanwhile employed the tactic in innovative ways. On 7 August 1998, al-Qaeda put itself on the map by destroying the American embassies in Kenya and Tanzania by means of two Hezbollah–like truck bomb attacks. Two years later, it copied a method previously employed by the LTTE, using a small boat loaded with explosives to attack the destroyer USS *Cole* in the port of Aden, Yemen. On 9 September 2001, two suicide bombers assassinated the leader of the Northern Alliance in Afghanistan by means of a bomb hidden in a camera – a strategic move that anticipated the consequences of the event planned for two days later: the 9/11 attacks.

Whereas the 9/11 attacks and the 'war on terror' that followed disrupted and further fragmented Osama bin Laden's network, it also inspired other organisations and groups to (at least partly) shift their attention to the global *jihad* and follow al-Qaeda's example. Accordingly, the years after 9/11 witnessed an increasing number of suicide attacks by groups and smaller cliques identifying with al-Qaeda. Suicide attacks were executed from Bali to London and from Riyadh to Casablanca, often against targets associated with the West. Yet it was in the conflict areas of Afghanistan, Iraq and Syria that suicide bombers would strike hardest.

In Afghanistan, suicide attacks had not been used during the Soviet invasion in the 1980s or during the Civil War of the 1990s. Since the American invasion of 2001, and particularly since 2005, however, the country has witnessed hundreds of suicide attacks by the Taliban as well as transnational jihadist groups, including al-Qaeda. These attacks primarily targeted coalition forces, Afghan military forces and policemen (Moghadam 2008: 152–8). The same development can be witnessed in neighbouring Pakistan, where both nationally oriented groups and transnational jihadist embraced the tactic against local authorities and military targets, as well as against the Shia Muslim community.

Nevertheless, it is Iraq that has become the main stage for suicide bombers. Suicide attacks were introduced in the country after the US-led invasion of 2003 and strongly increased in numbers in the years 2005–7, when resistance against the international forces and internal sectarian strife peaked. The large majority of suicide attacks in this period were carried out by transnational jihadists, most of whom belonged to al-Qaeda in Iraq (Hafez 2007: 106–9). They targeted both coalition forces and Iraqi military and policemen, as well as Shia Muslims. When resistance in Iraq diminished during the so-called Anbar Awakening, the numbers of suicide bombings also strongly declined. Yet they rose again to unprecedented heights when al-Qaeda in Iraq's successor, the Islamic State of Iraq and Syria (which changed its name into the Islamic State in 2014) started its conquests in the country in 2013. Combined with the outbreak of the Syrian Civil War in 2011 and the role of jihadist groups therein, the rise of the Islamic State has caused unparalleled numbers of suicide attacks in the region (Joscelyn 2016; Winter 2017).

In sum, according to the Global Terrorism Database (START 2018), a total of 6,633 suicide attacks had been executed between 1981 and the end of 2017.[4] The large majority of these attacks (70.6 per cent) took place in Iraq (2,602 attacks), Afghanistan (1,228), Pakistan (511) and Syria (344). The main perpetrators were the Islamic State in Iraq and Syria (1,314 attacks since 2013), the Afghan Taliban (716) and al-Qaeda and its official affiliates (356). Most targets were associated with military and police forces, governments and non-state militias (63.8 per cent), yet a significant number struck civilian targets.

---

[4] The Global Terrorism Database by the National Consortium for the Study of Terrorism and Responses to Terrorism (START) takes a broad definition of suicide attacks: it designates a terrorist attack as a suicide attack when there 'is evidence that the perpetrator did not intend to escape from the attack alive'. Plots involving multiple attacks are listed as multiple attacks (e.g. the 9/11 attacks count for four separate attacks).

Finally, the above overview clearly demonstrates the rise of suicide attacks after 9/11: from 216 attacks between 1981 and the 9/11 attacks to 6,417 in the period between 9/11 and the end of 2017 (START 2018). Moreover, the post–9/11 years witnessed a transformation of the phenomenon from a tactic employed by a restricted number of groups participating in local, predominantly ethnonationalist, asymmetric conflicts in the 1980s and 1990s to a transnational phenomenon used by a plethora of groups and cliques across the world that were often inspired by global jihadism. In this sense, we could indeed speak of a 'globalisation' of the suicide attack. This observation is also supported by the fact that relatively large numbers of suicide bombers in countries such as Afghanistan, Iraq and Syria were foreign fighters in these countries (Moghadam 2008: 156; Hafez 2007: 251–4). Nevertheless, the particular contexts that gave rise to the attacks, as well as the backgrounds, motivations and aims of the individual bombers and their organisations have remained highly diverse and are often still rooted in local political, social and cultural circumstances. This will be further explored in the next section by discussing how scholars have tried to make sense of the proliferation of suicide attacks in recent decades.

1.3 Explaining Suicide Attacks

Since the 9/11 attacks, the field of terrorism studies has witnessed exponential growth (Silke 2008). Not very surprisingly, this field has also dominated research on suicide attacks until now. As a result, most studies on the topic have been produced by scholars with backgrounds in terrorism studies, political science and, to a lesser extent, international relations, sociology and psychology. This becomes evident from current literature on the phenomenon, which typically approaches suicide attacks as a form of terrorism. To understand this form of terrorism, most scholars distinguish between three (interconnected) levels of analysis: organisations, individuals suicide bombers and the larger societies or communities of these actors (see Crenshaw 2007; Ward 2018). Nevertheless, they particularly emphasise the importance of organisations, generally agreeing with Martha Crenshaw's observation that 'the organization that recruits and directs the suicide bomber remains the most important agent' (2007: 157).

The remainder of this section will discuss the main findings of terrorism scholars regarding the roles of organisations and individual bombers. As it will demonstrate, the actions of these organisations and individuals can only be understood by situating them in their social environment. For this reason, this (alleged) third level of analysis will not be treated separately, but will rather be integrated into the discussion of the organisational and individual levels. In doing so, the role of religion will be largely left implicit, as this will be the topic of Section 2.

Organisations

One of the reasons for emphasising the role of organisations behind suicide attacks is that, at least until recently, the large majority of attacks have been carried out with the support of organisations (Pape 2006: 4; Gambetta 2005: 260). Scholars have typically considered suicide attacks 'a product of a strategic choice' for these organisations (Crenshaw 1998). Ami Pedahzur writes: 'suicide terrorism ... is a product of an organization's political strategy after it has defined its goals, clarified the options it has in order to realise these goals and checked the price label attached to each operational method' (2005: 27). Accordingly, rather than irrational or desperate behaviour, suicide attacks are typically seen as the product of a rational and calculated choice by organisations that consider it an effective means to reach their goals (Hoffman 2017: 140).

The tactical and operational benefits of suicide attacks are considered important in explaining why organisations make this choice (Hafez 2007: 9–14; Moghadam 2008: 31–2). Suicide attacks are deemed to be cost-efficient and, as the 'ultimate smart bomb', they are highly precise and relatively lethal. Moreover, even more than ordinary terrorist attacks, suicide attacks have a huge psychological impact on the targeted population. They are therefore a powerful tool in psychological warfare, and are likely to draw much media attention. This media attention may help organisations to bring their cause to the attention of the targeted public. Hence, suicide attacks have been described as a form of strategic communication or as 'strategic signalling' (Hoffman and McCormick 2004) through which an organisation calls attention to its character and goals. Other scholars have interpreted suicide attacks as performances that are designed to make an impact on the audience

(Alexander 2004). These performances are considered to be effective because, through their attacks, the bombers demonstrate their willingness to sacrifice themselves for the group's cause, which may enhance the legitimacy of the organisation in the eyes of its supporters and potential recruits.

These tactical and operational benefits already indicate that suicide attacks may be beneficial for organisations in two ways: by weakening the opponent and strengthening the own group. A prominent example of an author emphasising the former is Robert A. Pape (2006; Pape and Feldman 2010). Pape argues that nearly all suicide attacks have a specific strategic goal in common: national liberation from foreign military occupation by democratic states (2006: 4). Suicide attacks have been relatively successful in achieving this goal in contexts of asymmetric conflict, Pape claims, which explains their spread across the world. A prominent scholar emphasising that organisations adopt suicide attacks to strengthen their own group is Mia M. Bloom (2005). While partly subscribing to Pape's thesis, Bloom adds that suicide attacks are also attractive because they enhance an organisation's prestige. They enable the organisation to increase its public support, which is particularly important in a context of intra-communal competition between groups. Bloom's so-called outbidding theory thus primarily interprets suicide attacks as part of local power struggles, perceiving them as a means for organisations to increase their 'market share' among the population they claim to represent.

Although these theories shed light on the use of suicide attacks in some cases, they have been criticised for offering explanations of the phenomenon that are too general. Pape's thesis that suicide attacks are predominantly a response to foreign occupation needs be taken into account when examining the cases of, for example, Hezbollah, the LTTE and Hamas. However, several authors have pointed out the limitations of his theory with regard to suicide attacks by jihadist groups (Atran 2006; Moghadam 2006a; Crenshaw 2007: 142–5; Hafez 2007: 213–15; Ward 2018: 99–100). Pape underestimates the role of religion, and especially Salafi jihadism, in this respect, they claim. Moreover, suicide attacks in Pakistan, as well as attacks executed by foreign fighters in countries such as Afghanistan, Iraq and Syria, are hard to explain as a response to foreign occupation. Hence, Pape's thesis is criticised for disregarding the globalisation of suicide attacks in the twenty-first century. Bloom's 'outbidding theory' is also considered important for interpreting suicide attacks in some contexts. Most evident is probably the case of the Palestinians during the al-Aqsa Intifada, for which she convincingly argues that internal competition between different Palestinian groups played a role in their decision to adopt the tactic (Bloom 2004). With regard to Sri Lanka, however, the 'outbidding theory' is less convincing, while it is considered even more problematic as an explanation of al-Qaeda's suicide attacks in terms of competition with rivals (Crenshaw 2007: 146; Hafez 2007: 216–17; Moghadam 2008: 36–7; Ward 2018: 99).

These criticisms of Pape and Bloom illustrate that general explanations for suicide attacks are now largely rejected. Instead, the strategic objectives of organisations *in their particular political contexts* are being emphasised (see also Gill 2013). In his extensive study of suicide attacks in Iraq since 2003, for example, Mohammed M. Hafez concludes that suicide attacks in this context became a tool for jihadists to spark sectarian violence and collapse an emerging democratic order (2006c; 2007: 225). About a decade later, suicide attacks in the region often had different objectives, however, as Charlie Winter (2017) demonstrates in his study on suicide attacks by the Islamic State. This group predominantly employed the means in order to defend its self-proclaimed caliphate. Rather than using suicide attacks as a form of terrorism, as had usually been the case in the preceding decades, the Islamic State used its 'martyr-dom machine' primarily as part of its battlefield tactics, typically employing fortified bomb cars and trucks in combination with more conventional forms of warfare.

Accordingly, current research from the field of terrorism studies largely agrees that (i) organisations are crucial to explain the phenomenon of suicide attacks, (ii) these organisations make a rational, strategic calculation to adopt suicide attacks and (iii) this calculation is made in and is dependent on specific political contexts, which are often dominated by asymmetrical military conflicts. In addition, most scholars agree that individual suicide attackers are motivated by other, largely non-strategic motivations (Hafez 2006a), as will be seen in the next section.

Individuals

In his discussion of suicide bombing, Talal Asad (2007: 39–64) rightly remarks that human motivations are far more complicated than is commonly supposed. They are often not even clear to the actors themselves, which raises questions about our capability to make sense of them. Nevertheless, terrorism researchers have provided significant insights into individual suicide bombers, the most important of which is that they are motivated by a wide range of factors that are strongly dependent on their particular backgrounds and environments (Crenshaw 2007: 153–4; Ward 2018: 90). As noted above, to explain why individuals engage in suicide attacks, researchers typically distinguish between three levels: the individuals themselves, their direct social networks and their larger societies and communities.

With regard to the bombers themselves, research has convincingly shown that their backgrounds are widely diverse. Contrary to popular misconceptions, they 'are not mainly poor, uneducated, immature religious zealots or social losers' (Pape 2006: 216). Thus, while the majority are young, male and Muslim, suicide bombers do not fit a common demographic profile (Atran 2003: 1536–7; Pape 2006: 199–216; Hafez 2007: 8; Moghadam 2008: 27; Ward 2018: 90). In this respect it is also interesting to note that the number of female suicide bombers has increased over the last two decades. While the use of female bombers remained largely limited to the LTTE, the PKK and Palestinian and Chechen groups until the mid-2000s, recent years also witnessed successful attacks by groups such as Boko Haram, al-Shabab and the Taliban. The reason for the increased use of female suicide bombers is usually sought in tactical and strategic factors (Bloom 2007; Speckhard 2008; Turner 2016).

In addition, research has found no conclusive evidence of specific psychological profiles or personality types characterising suicide attackers. Some early studies attributed suicide attacks to psychopathology, but recent research largely dismisses mental illness or personality disorders as an explanation for terrorism in general and suicide attacks in particular (Silke 1998; Victoroff 2005; Post 2007; Horgan 2014: 47–76). Furthermore, although suicide bombers have been labelled as narcissistic, paranoid, antisocial and introvert, there is little hard evidence that they have a particular personality type or distinctive personality traits (Ward 2018: 93–9). Hence, suicide bombers are generally considered normal with regard to their psychological profile.

Rather than looking for commonalities in demographic and psychological profiles, many scholars argue that attention should be shifted to the particular backgrounds and life courses of suicide attackers. Relatively large numbers of suicide attackers are found to have experienced a personal crisis in the period before their attack, for instance because they have lost a relative or friend, experienced financial problems or witnessed a traumatic event (Pedahzur 2005: 134–42). These experiences might result in a desire for revenge, which can motivate violence. Some studies argue that many female bombers in particular have gone through a personal crisis, which often has to do with expected social roles and perceptions of honour and shame. Cases of divorce, rape or unintended pregnancy are often mentioned (Victor 2003; Bloom 2005: 142–65). Other authors have disagreed, however, arguing that these explanations are based on stereotyped gender roles in which women are denied agency (Brunner 2007; Marway 2015); personal crises are significant, these authors claim, but not necessarily related to gender. They argue that the motivations of female bombers are very similar to those of men (Speckhard and Ahkmedova 2006: 475; Speckhard 2008).

Finally, researchers have argued convincingly that the motivations of suicide bombers cannot be compared to those of ordinary suicides who wish to die in order to put an end to intolerable mental pain (Merari 2010: 222). Several scholars have used Émile Durkheim's (1897) categories of altruistic and fatalistic suicide to interpret the death of suicide attackers (Pape 2005: 171–9; Pedahzur 2005: 6–8; Graitl 2017). From this perspective, suicide is explained by relating it to the individual's societal environment, and thus to issues such as social conditions and the societal approval of violence. Due to the lack of evidence regarding demographic and psychological profiles, it is this societal environment that has become central to most interpretations of the motivations of suicide bombers.

On the one hand, the direct social environment is considered significant. Suicide bombers hardly act alone. Until 9/11, the large majority were part of formal organisations such as Hezbollah, Hamas and the LTTE, which either recruited them or to which they volunteered to execute a suicide mission (Pedahzur 2005; Pape 2006). In the years after 9/11, formal organisations were relatively less involved, especially in the case of global jihadists. The war on terror following 9/11 further fragmented the jihadist movement, also because organisations and smaller groups from across the world started to identify with al-Qaeda's global *jihad*. As a result, the years since 9/11 have witnessed increasing numbers of attacks executed by small cells or cliques that might have been inspired, but were not recruited and/or directed by formal organisations (e.g. Pedahzur and Perliger 2006; Kirby 2007). Yet social bonds, and especially family and friendship ties, have remained crucial factors in explaining radicalisation and suicide attacks both in conflict areas and beyond (Sageman 2004, 2008; Atran 2006; Roy 2017). The concept of 'lone wolves', which has gained prominence in recent years in relation to attacks inspired by groups such as al-Qaeda and the Islamic State, has come under increasing criticism (e.g. Schuurman et al. 2018). Accordingly, the individual's commitment to the group, often in combination with peer pressure, is considered important in understanding individual suicide bombers, both in the cases of formal organisations and informal cliques (Pedahzur 2005: 126–34, 155–81).

On the other hand, the larger society and community of suicide bombers are considered important. With regard to the political context, it is evident that armed conflicts provide a favourable environment for the occurrence of suicide attacks, especially when one of the parties feels marginalised or oppressed (e.g. Hafez 2007). Situations of oppression and injustice might lead to perceptions of humiliation, which is often mentioned as a prime motive for suicide attackers. Feelings of humiliation can come in two forms, Farhad Khosrokhavar (2005: 152–3) indicates: one might experience personal humiliation directly in daily life or indirectly through the group one identifies with (i.e. 'humiliation by proxy'). While the former is often found in conflict areas such as Lebanon, Palestine and Chechnya, the latter is particularly important in the case of transnational jihadists, for whom identification with the (suffering) worldwide Muslim community (*umma*) is often crucial in their decision to join the global *jihad*. In both cases, perceived humiliation might trigger a desire for revenge, which is considered a significant motivation for suicide attacks (Stern 2003; Speckhard and Ahkmedova 2006; Hafez 2007; Moghadam 2008; Singh 2011;).

The role of economic variables is debated. According to some authors, issues such as poverty and lack of education increase the risk of suicide attacks, but others resist a direct connection between economic grievances and suicide attacks (see Atran 2003: 1536–7; Pedahzur 2005: 134–7; Moghadam 2008: 33). What most authors do agree on is that the socio-cultural environment is crucial: social support for suicide attacks is one of the most significant variables explaining why individuals engage in this form of violence (Crenshaw 2007: 149–53). In places such as Lebanon and Palestine, a so-called cult of martyrdom was deliberately cultivated by organisations to increase support for their actions. This strategy was effective due to the contexts of (perceived) threats and feelings of victimisation among the population (Hafez 2006b: 53–65; Pedahzur 2005: 158–64). Yet cultures of martyrdom also emerged within smaller networks. Among transnational jihadists, for example, an ethos of martyrdom has developed since the 1980s. Nurtured by the comprehensive propaganda efforts of jihadist organisations, the (often online) celebration of martyrdom and 'martyrdom seekers' has provided a fertile context for the production of suicide bombers (Hafez 2007; Moghadam 2008; Nanninga 2014). Martyrdom cultures like these provide rationale and meaning to suicide attacks for individuals.

To summarise, research has demonstrated that there are no general explanations for the phenomenon of suicide attacks. The current literature underlines that it is crucial to distinguish between the levels of the organisation and the individual and to acknowledge that both of these actors are motivated by a mix of factors that is strongly dependent on concrete circumstances, in which political factors such as occupation, competition and oppression are deemed to be particularly important. Any attempt to understand the phenomenon of suicide attacks therefore requires a multidimensional and contextual approach.

2 Religion and Suicide Attacks

The role of religion in suicide attacks has been largely left implicit so far. As noted above, research on suicide attacks has hitherto been mainly dominated by terrorism scholars, for whom religion is usually not a prime interest. Nevertheless, they typically acknowledge its significance. This section will therefore start by providing an overview of current interpretations of the role of religion in suicide attacks. Subsequently, it will relate these interpretations to insights from the field of religious studies and related fields and disciplines. Based on these insights, this section will identify some challenges regarding current interpretations of the role of religion in suicide attacks, after which it concludes by proposing a more nuanced approach to the topic. This approach will then guide the exploration of the role of Islam in suicide attacks in Section 3.

2.1 Existing Explanations of the Role of Religion

Researchers rightly refute the perception that suicide attacks are either a 'fundamentally religious' or a 'typically Islamic' phenomenon (e.g. Weinberg 2006). As we have noted, secular groups such as the PKK and the LTTE used suicide attacks as part of their ethnonationalist struggles. Moreover, conflicts in which religion was involved have also produced suicide attacks by secular groups, such as the Syrian Social Nationalist Party in Lebanon, the PFLP in Palestine and (former) Ba'athist networks in Iraq. Besides, most authors agree that in cases in which religion is involved, it is never the sole motivating factor. Hence, religion is considered neither a necessary nor a sufficient condition for suicide attacks (Crenshaw 2007: 149).

Nevertheless, terrorism researchers agree that religion, and Islam in particular, has played a crucial role in the suicide attacks that have been committed in recent decades (Ward 2018: 91). Several particular functions of religion have been identified, which can be categorised according to the above-mentioned three levels of analysis: individuals, organisations and societies.

First, religion is considered to provide legitimation and meaning to suicide attacks for individual suicide bombers. Moghadam, for example, claims that Salafi jihadism shapes the mental framework of jihadist suicide bombers, which enables them to justify and rationalise their actions. It offers them a world view that is characterised by a good versus evil dichotomy, dehumanises their enemies and morally disengages them from their actions (Moghadam 2008: 254–5). A related element that is often mentioned in relation to individual bombers is the rewards (allegedly) promised to martyrs in Islamic traditions, including the well-known virgins of Paradise and the possibility of intercession for relatives (e.g. Pedahzur 2005: 37–8; Moghadam 2008: 29). These rewards, it is argued, might play a role in suicide bombers individual cost-benefit calculations. They offer individuals the 'ultimate benefit' and, as such, religion may facilitate the overcoming of day-to-day injustice and humiliation through martyrdom (Khosrokhavar 2005: 133–4).

Second, researchers point out the ways in which religion is used in an instrumental way by organisations to justify violence, mobilise support and train recruits. Ami Pedahzur (2005: 165–80) claims that organisations from different regions have used Islamic martyrdom traditions to convince people of the legitimacy and necessity of suicide attacks and to ensure that recruits are (ideologically) committed to their task. Mohammed Hafez (2006a) argues that Palestinian organisations have strategically used religious traditions to engender the culture of martyrdom that has underpinned their suicide attacks against Israel. Hamas and Islamic Jihad have strategically drawn from *jihad* and martyrdom traditions as well as ritual and ceremony to foster a culture venerating suicide bombers. Iraqi organisations have followed the same strategy, Hafez (2007: 218–21) argues in another study. Although the motivations of these organisations have been diverse and their rhetoric has not been exclusively religious, Islamic traditions have been crucial in their attempts to legitimise their violence and mobilise support.

Third, several studies emphasise the role of religion at the societal level, arguing that it may strengthen social ties within a society at large or within particular communities or groups (see Ward 2018: 101–2; Ginges, Hansen and Norenzayan 2009). Religion can facilitate the creation of a strong collective identity and thus a high commitment to these collectives by individual members, which is important given the importance of social ties and group commitment as a motivation for suicide attacks. According to some studies on jihadist networks and cliques, social connections, such as friendship and kinship bonds, are key in explaining why youngsters join the jihadist movement (e.g. Sageman 2004, 2008; Kirby 2007). Yet the role of (specific interpretations of) Islam is considered crucial for strengthening these bonds, creating commitment and adopting new values that stimulate in-group love and out-group hatred. These issues may eventually be a strong incentive for violence. For example, Mark Sageman writes that, while the violence of global jihadists is grounded in social relations and dynamics, their specific version of Islam 'feeds on this natural and intense loyalty to the group and transforms alienated young Muslims into fanatical terrorists' (2006: 131).

Based on these insights, several authors have assessed the significance of religion as compared to other (allegedly) secular factors, such as political and socio-economic ones. A prominent example in this respect is Robert A. Pape, as well as some of his critics. As noted above, Pape emphasises the role of foreign occupation, while claiming that 'the data show that there is little connection between suicide terrorism and Islamic fundamentalism, or any of the world's religions'. Hence, he argues, 'religion is rarely the root cause, although it is often used as a tool by terrorist organizations in recruiting and in other efforts in service of the broader strategic objective' (Pape 2006: 4). Others disagree, however, emphasising the crucial role of religion in the proliferation of suicide attacks over recent years. Moghadam emphasises the role of Salafi jihadism in the rise and spread of suicide attacks in the twenty-first century, arguing that it 'provided the much needed theological, religious, and moral justification' for suicide attacks in different contexts (Moghadam 2008: 253). A more specific example is provided by the case of Chechnya, where jihadism is considered crucial for the introduction of suicide attacks. In the Chechen conflict, suicide attacks were introduced only after (a more nationalist form of) jihadism was adopted around 2000. According to Anne Speckhard and Khapta Akhmedova (2006), the adoption of this ideology resulted in a 'lethal mix' of traumatic experiences and a desire for revenge in combination with groups offering both the ideology and means for suicide operations. These studies illustrate that most researchers agree that religion has been *part of* the motivations for the majority suicide attacks. However, they disagree about its primacy relative to other factors.

Other scholars go a step further by (either implicitly or explicitly) distinguishing between attacks that are motivated by religion and attacks that are motivated by secular causes, such as ethnonationalism (e.g. Bloom 2006). These attacks are different in nature, it is implied, which is mainly due to the different mindset of the actors. Religious actors typically perceive violence as a sacred duty in the context of a holy war, these studies assert, which is characterised by a drive for purification, a celebration of martyrdom and millennialist or apocalyptic beliefs (e.g. Hoffman 2017: 83–138). Perceptions like these are claimed to impact the behaviour of organisations and individuals. For example, they make religious actors harder to negotiate with than secular actors, who are presumed to be more pragmatic. These perceptions may also play a role in religious actors' decision to adopt suicide attacks. With regard to Somalia, for example, religion is considered a prime explanation for the fact that only al-Shabab adopted suicide attacks in the mid-2000s, while other Somali insurgency groups did not (Hansen 2011). Moreover, in line with findings on terrorism in general (Hoffman 1995), some authors claim that the above beliefs cause suicide attacks by religious actors to be more lethal and destructive than those by secular groups (e.g. Henne 2012).

In short, religion seems to fulfil some specific functions on the levels of the individual bombers and their organisations and social environments, such as providing moral justification, offering rewards, facilitating recruitment, creating social cohesion and galvanising social support. However, the significance of religion relative to other factors is a topic of scholarly debate.

2.2 Problematising the Role of Religion

These conclusions illustrate that current research on suicide attacks has delivered important insights into the phenomenon. Most prominently, by emphasising the strategic use of the means as well as the 'normalcy' of suicide bombers, researchers have convincingly countered widespread perceptions of suicide bombers as fanatical zealots and psychopaths. Nevertheless, research on suicide attacks also faces some challenges, especially with regard to interpreting the role of religion. Based on insights from the field of religious studies and related fields and disciplines, two major challenges can be distinguished: a lack of conceptualisation and a lack of contextualisation of religion.

Religion and 'the Secular'

Many studies on suicide attacks straightforwardly distinguish between the religious and the non-religious, often labelled as 'the secular'. They do so on two levels. Some researchers distinguish religiously motivated suicide attacks from their secular counterparts; others distinguish between religious and secular *factors* underlying the use of suicide attacks. Recent research in the field of religious studies raises some critical questions about these distinctions.

First, one might wonder whether it is fruitful to distinguish between religiously motivated suicide attacks and those allegedly conducted for secular causes. As already noted, suicide attacks are never motivated by religion alone. In cases in which religion is involved, there is always an interplay between religion and other factors, such as political, social and cultural ones. This perspective is underscored by religious studies scholars, for whom the relationship between religion and violence has become a major research subject in the twenty-first century. Mark Juergensmeyer, for example, emphasises the importance of studying religion in relation to other factors in order to understand its role in 'religious terrorism'. Religion does not ordinarily lead to violence, he claims: 'This happens only with the coalescence of a particular set of circumstances – political, social, and ideological – when religion becomes fused with violent expressions of social aspirations, personal pride, and movements for political change' (Juergensmeyer 2003: 10). R. Scott Appleby (2000) also emphasises the importance of contextualising religion. When one does so, it becomes evident that the role of religion in violence is ambiguous, he argues: under some circumstances, people's encounter with 'the sacred' may fuel violence, while in other contexts religion may contribute to reconciliation and peace-building. Hence, the role of religion in violence can only be understood when acknowledging its entanglement with other factors.

This raises questions about typologies that distinguish between religiously motivated suicide attacks and their secular counterparts. To put it more precisely, such distinctions break down under close empirical examination (Jackson et al. 2011: 161–3). The suicide attacks by Hamas, for example, are often seen as religiously motivated as opposed to those by groups such as the secular PFLP. However, Hamas evidently combines religious and nationalist elements in its ideology, rhetoric and practices. Its goal of liberating Palestine from Israeli occupation, for example, can be classified as both nationalist and religious. Moreover, the strategies used by

Hamas to accomplish this goal have often been highly pragmatic rather than driven by religious principles (Mishal and Sela 2006; Gunning 2009). This raises questions about the usefulness of singling out one aspect of Hamas's ideology (i.e. religion) to categorise the group's actions.

The LTTE provides an example in the opposite direction. While the attacks executed by the Tamil Tigers are typically categorised as secular, the group's rhetoric regarding suicide attacks was immersed in religious discourse. The attacks were strongly ritualised and the LTTE drew from Hindu traditions of self-sacrifice, asceticism and rebirth to give meaning to them and to promote a culture of martyrdom, which became firmly established among its supporters in Sri Lankan society (Schalk 1997; Roberts 2005; Schalk 2017). These cases thus raise questions concerning the criteria that should be used to classify the attacks by Hamas and the LTTE as either religious or secular (cf. Gunning and Jackson 2011: 376–8). Are the organisation's ideology, rhetoric and goals defining in this respect? How should one prioritise religious and non-religious aspects when both are involved? These questions illustrate that the opposition between religious and non-religious suicide attacks needs critical reflection. Such a categorisation runs the risk of prioritising religion over other factors, implying that it plays a defining role and makes suicide attacks by religious actors fundamentally different from those by actors (allegedly) motivated by other ideologies.

In addition, distinctions between religious and non-religious *factors* underlying the use of suicide attacks need to be examined carefully, since they are often hard to separate. In the field of religious studies, the boundaries between the religious and the secular are increasingly challenged (see Nanninga 2019). Building on the work of Talal Asad (1993; 2003) and others, several scholars studying religion and violence claim that it is impossible to provide a clear, universal definition of religion. Conceptions of religion diverge over time and place – they are historically produced, reproduced and transformed. Our conceptualisation of the religious as opposed to the secular, for example, is a product of political and social processes in the modern Western world, such as the rise of the modern nation state and the privatisation of religion. For this reason, they argue that there are no objective criteria to determine what constitutes 'religion' and what does not. This makes it problematic to straightforwardly distinguish between 'religious violence' and its secular counterpart or between religious and non-religious causes of suicide attacks (Cavanaugh 2009; Gunning and Jackson 2011). This has consequences for the discussion of the role of religion in suicide attacks, as the case of al-Qaeda illustrates.[5]

Over the last two decades, al-Qaeda has issued several criticisms of the West in order to legitimise its struggle. In his 2002 'Letter to the American people', for example, Bin Laden emphasises Western support for Israel, Russia and India in the slaughter of Muslims in Palestine, Chechnya and Kashmir, respectively. Moreover, he indicates that Americans 'steal our wealth and oil', collaborate with governments in the Middle East that are oppressing Muslims and actively starve Muslims in Iraq through their sanctions against the Saddam Hussein regime. Western morality is corrupted according to the al-Qaeda leader, which he further illustrates by pointing out its negligence of usury, intoxicants and gambling, its exploitation of women, its destruction of nature and its 'hypocrisy in manners and principles' that has become evident throughout history – from Hiroshima to Guantánamo (Bin Laden 2002).

Al-Qaeda thus provides various reasons for its war against the West. Seemingly 'religious' arguments are being used side by side with arguments that we could label 'historical', 'political' and 'economic'. To put it more precisely, these 'religious' and 'non-religious' factors are strongly intertwined and difficult to separate consistently. The case of foreign occupation illustrates this point.

The (alleged) Western occupation of Muslims lands, and especially the presence of US troops in Saudi Arabia since the Gulf War of 1990–1, has been one of al-Qaeda's prime charges against the West. Regarding Saudi Arabia, Bin Laden and his associates wrote as early as 1998 that the USA was 'plundering its riches, dictating to its rulers, humiliating its people, terrorising its neighbours and turning its bases in the Peninsula into a spearhead through which to fight the neighbouring Muslim peoples' (World Islamic Front 1998). Presupposing the religious-secular divide that is dominant in Western discourse today, this formulation could lead

---

[5] A more elaborate version of this example can be found in Nanninga (2017).

us to the conclusion that the 'occupation' of Saudi Arabia should be considered a non-religious (i.e. political, economic) argument for al-Qaeda's resistance against the West. This is indeed what Robert A. Pape (2006) argues in his analysis of al-Qaeda's suicide attacks. Others disagree, however, because, from al-Qaeda's perspective, the occupation of the Arabian Peninsula is a thoroughly religious issue (e.g. Moghadam 2006a). Drawing from authoritative Islamic jurisprudence on *jihad* (see Cook 2005), al-Qaeda argues that the waging of *jihad* is an individual duty for each Muslim in order to liberate Muslim lands from occupation by unbelievers. Accordingly, Bin Laden states in his letter to the Americans: 'Allah, the Almighty, legislated the permission and the option to take revenge. Thus, if we are attacked, then we have the right to attack back'. This is 'commanded by our religion', he warns the Americans, so 'do not await anything from us but Jihad, resistance and revenge' (Bin Laden 2002).

The question thus arises whether occupation should be considered a 'religious' legitimation of al-Qaeda's violence or not. On the one hand, al-Qaeda's self-understanding on this point needs to be taken seriously. The fact that Bin Laden frames al-Qaeda's actions as a religiously sanctioned *jihad* is important to understanding al-Qaeda's violence. On the other hand, however, Bin Laden's framing of the events in religious language should not be taken at face value. First of all, these framing efforts do not necessarily imply that religion is central to the motivations of the organisers and perpetrators of al-Qaeda's violence. There is a need for closer examination of the role of these perceptions in al-Qaeda's decision-making as well as in the motivations of individual perpetrators. In addition, the question of whether occupation constitutes a religious or a secular incentive for violence is problematic from an analytical point of view, as it mistakenly presupposes a clear, unambiguous distinction between a 'religious' and a 'secular' sphere. Hence, although the presence of US troops in Saudi Arabia and Bin Laden's framing of this in religious language have arguably contributed to al-Qaeda's actions, any conclusion as to whether this makes al-Qaeda's attacks 'religious' is not very helpful.

In sum, religious and non-religious factors are closely intertwined and hard to separate. Yet suspending the rigid religion-secular divide that dominates much of the literature on suicide attacks does not imply that the concept of religion itself should be completely abandoned. Rather, as Gunning and Jackson (2011) argue, the concept should be problematised and historicised in order to avoid rigid typologies that *a priori* prioritise some factors over others. This also illustrates that making general claims about the role of religion (as an abstract category) in suicide attacks is not very helpful. Instead, what is needed is careful, empirically based research on how particular constructs of beliefs, values and attitudes – labelled religious or otherwise – are being used to shape, motivate and give meaning to violence. Such an approach shifts the focus to the practising of religion in concrete situations. It is here that a second challenge to existing research on suicide attacks becomes visible.

Religion and Culture

Due to the dominance of terrorism scholars, research on suicide attacks has mainly focused on their political context and, to a lesser extent, on the socio-economic and psychological backgrounds of the perpetrators. What has remained understudied so far is the cultural context of the phenomenon. Except for some descriptions of so-called cultures of martyrdom, especially in Palestine, terrorism scholars have, in the words of cultural anthropologist David B. Edwards, 'largely ignored the cultural matrix out of which this practice has arisen' (2017: 129). Yet it is crucial to take into account cultural factors to understand the phenomenon, Edwards claims. Many researchers, for example, suggest that feelings of humiliation are a crucial motivation for suicide attacks, because humiliation is a central theme in the statements of many suicide bombers themselves. However, Edwards indicates, without examining the cultural context of the practice, we cannot know whether the English term 'humiliation' captures the meaning of the terms the perpetrators use, nor can we know how these feelings have come about and why they lead to particular responses (2017: 142). Hence, he states, 'there are commonalities in the practice of suicide bombing across cultures', but we should not only focus on these commonalities, as they tend 'to overshadow the particular ways in which practice relates to culture and place and, in the case of suicide bombing, how it has both affected and been affected by the culture in which it is now embedded' (Edwards 2017: 214).

There is an additional reason for embedding suicide attacks in their cultural context. Due to the current focus on the political background of suicide attacks, many studies have aimed to explain the phenomenon by (predominantly) perceiving it in instrumental terms: as a means to certain ends. Yet this 'rationalist paradigm', as Mohammed Hafez (2006a) calls it, is insufficient to fully grasp the phenomenon. Scott Atran (2006: 138–9), for example, writes that the values of the suicide bombers he interviewed were not entirely sensitive to standard political or economic calculations. He claims that the 'power of faith' and cultural values such as honour might ultimately lead to perceived moral obligations that appear to be irrational, such as self-sacrifice for a certain cause. Moreover, suicide attacks are not just a utilitarian practice, they also have meanings for the actors involved. They can also be seen as expressive forms of social action that 'say' something to their audiences (Davis 1973; Blok 2001b). This perspective finds its origins in Clifford Geertz's interpretative approach to social action. In his famous essay on Balinese cockfights, Geertz (1973b) describes a social practice in which, from a utilitarian point of view, the stakes are so high that it seems irrational for people to participate in it. However, Geertz argued, attention must be drawn to the expressive, theatrical aspects and meanings of the practices, which he did by analysing the cockfights as a text: 'a story they tell themselves about themselves' (Geertz 1973b: 448). In making comprehensible the structure of Balinese society and their incorporation of central themes of Balinese life such as honour, prestige, status, humiliation, kinship and conflict, cockfights can be viewed as performances of life on the island itself, he argued.

Although Geertz has been criticised for largely overlooking people's agency and the flexibility as well as the performative impact of cultural practices, his approach demonstrates the significance of embedding suicide attacks in their cultural context to be able to fully grasp the phenomenon. This is illustrated by Rashmi Singh's multilevel analysis of Hamas's suicide attacks, which shows that they are not merely a strategic means based on rational calculations. Organisations such as Hamas are produced by and embedded in a particular cultural context, Singh claims, which also shapes their actions, as she illustrates by means of the cultural norm of militant heroic martyrdom that is entrenched in Palestinian society. In addition to being an instrumental means, Hamas's suicide attacks are therefore also a form of expressive violence that conveys symbolic messages to various audiences (Singh 2011). Singh's study illustrates that the 'rationalist paradigm' dominating current research on suicide attacks has to be supplemented by studies focusing on the cultural context in order to understand the *meanings* that perpetrators, organisers and supporters attribute to these actions. Hafez writes: 'We have yet to encounter many studies that seek to *understand* the social meaning of martyrdom for the actors involved. How do suicide bombers view their actions? What meanings do they give to their sacrifice?' (2006a: 54).

Comprehensive studies of the cultural contexts that have given rise to suicide attacks are still largely lacking. This has consequences for how the role of religion is approached. Without paying close attention to the cultural contexts of suicide attacks, there is a risk of perceiving religion, or particular religious traditions such as Islam, as a separate 'force' that exist independently from the particular historical and cultural settings in which it is being practised. Religion becomes a static, unchanging variable, typically in the form of a (fixed) set of texts and doctrines that impacts, or even determines, the behaviour of its practitioners. In other words, without embedding religious traditions in the diverse and dynamic contexts in which they are being practised, religion is easily reified.

Essentialist perceptions of religion are indeed encountered in the literature on suicide attacks, albeit often in subtle and nuanced forms. Many studies addressing the role of religion predominantly point out the role of Islamic martyrdom traditions, typically discussing passages from the Qur'an and *hadith* collections as well as references to these traditions by contemporary ideologues, organisations and suicide bombers. The implication is that these (textual) traditions are central to the beliefs of suicide bombers and their supporters, and therefore explain their behaviour. However, the classical texts themselves are not that significant to understanding suicide attacks. Rather, it is crucial how they are interpreted and experienced by contemporary believers to grasp their influence. As Olivier Roy somewhat provocatively states: 'The mistake here is to focus on theology and therefore on the texts'. What is largely disregarded, he continues, is what he calls 'religiosity': the way in which believers experience religion and appropriate elements of theology, practices, imaginaries and rites (Roy 2017: 41–2). Hence, what is needed is in-depth examination of how these traditions are being appropriated, reinterpreted and transformed by suicide bombers in the highly diverse cultural contexts in the Muslim world and beyond.

In sum, although current research has delivered important insights into the role of religion in suicide attacks, input from scholars of religious studies and related fields and disciplines could further our understanding of the topic. First, much of the literature distinguishes between religious and secular suicide attacks and debates the primacy of religion as compared to other factors, but it might be more fruitful to focus on the entanglement of (alleged) religious and non-religious factors and thus on how and under which circumstances particular combinations of these factors give rise to suicide attacks. Second, in-depth research on the cultural context of suicide attacks will enable analysis of suicide attacks as expressive practices and thus deepen our understanding of the meanings of these attacks for perpetrators and organisers. Third, this will also provide a more nuanced view on the role of religious traditions in suicide attacks – not as a fixed 'thing' that exists 'out there' and simply impacts the behaviour of people through texts and doctrines, but rather as a dynamic phenomenon that is constantly being reinterpreted and transformed by believers in their particular and ever-changing historical and cultural contexts.

2.3 *Approaching Religion and Suicide Attacks*

Such an approach thus focuses on the *practising* of religion, which is also advocated by many religious studies scholars (e.g. Malory 1999). This also implies a contextualised approach to religion, as it is only by embedding religion in its concrete historical and cultural circumstances that we can begin to understand the highly diverse ways in which people have used religious traditions to give meaning to their lives and the world around them. Along these lines, religious studies scholars typically study religion as *part of* culture, that is as part of the historically transmitted, learned and shared 'pattern of meaning embodied in symbols' by means of which 'men communicate, perpetuate and develop their knowledge about and attitudes towards life' (Geertz 1973a: 89). Hence, both (alleged) 'religious' carriers of meaning, such as particular texts, beliefs, stories and rituals, and public symbols and symbolic acts that are commonly perceived as secular, can be perceived as part of the cultural repertoires through which people experience, express and shape meaning.

A useful way to conceptualise culture (and religion as part thereof) along these lines is to imagine it as a repertoire or 'toolkit' which people use in varying configurations to make sense of and act on the world (Swidler 1986: 273). According to Ann Swidler, one of the pioneering advocates of the culture-as-toolkit metaphor, cultures provide socially transmitted tools such as symbols, stories, rituals and world views that are cultivated in and learned by their users. Culture thus plays a constitutive role and influences (and restrains) people's actions by providing materials out of which people can build patterns of action. However, rather than perceiving people as 'products of culture', the metaphor of the toolkit emphasises people's agency. It shifts the focus of analysis to how people *use* the cultural tools available to them in diverse and complex ways in different settings (Swidler 2001: 24–40). In doing so, the toolkit metaphor also underlines that cultures are dynamic rather than static. People use their cultural resources creatively, selecting different tools and using them in diverse ways. Moreover, when the situation changes, existing tools might be used in novel ways and new tools might be invented or appropriated from other repertoires, while old tools gradually fall out of use. Hence, although culture is often presented as being fixed by its practitioners, the toolkit metaphor suggests that it is actually flexible and that its users actively contribute to its construction.

To provide an illustrative example of this perspective, religious leaders may appropriate certain texts and narratives referring to a perceived glorious and 'pure' period from the past in order to portray their movement as a restoration of this era. Hence, they attempt to authorise their views and empower their supporters by representing their movement as in line with the 'essence' or fundamental characteristics of their religious tradition (see Eickelman and James Piscatori 2004: 22–45). Essentialist perspectives like these are understandable, because they offer a clear-cut image of reality, construct collective identifications and enable leaders to justify their actions by claiming a direct continuity with a glorified past. However, cultures and religious traditions are not as static as they are often presented to be. By claiming to revive an imagined golden period from the past, these leaders may actually (attempt to) authorise new practices or beliefs and mobilise their community. Appealing to historical traditions and symbols from the past then becomes a vehicle for change. As a result, expressions of essentialist perspectives like these are actually part of the (re)construction of culture and religion (Baumann 1999: 91–2). Hence, according to this processual perspective, people are not only shaped by culture, they also (re)produce it.

This also implies that the cultural toolkit metaphor acknowledges culture's diversity. People use the cultural repertoires at their disposal in different ways. They master different tools and use different parts of the repertoire, also because they have unequal access to the cultural repertoire due to their different social positions (see Lamont 1992; Lamont and Thévenot 2000). Moreover, people use the same tools in varying ways, as a result of which cultural tools are often contested. Finally, it is significant to realise that people are not stuck in a single culture. Rather, they have different cultural resources at their disposal, depending on the various sociocultural settings they engage in and thus on issues such as national, ethnic, tribal and religious identifications. People constantly shift among multiple cultural realities, creatively drawing from the cultural resources available to them (Swidler 2001: 40).

Conceptualising culture (and religion as part of it) along these lines also sheds light on the relation between culture and actions, which is relevant for our exploration of the relationship between Islam and suicide attacks. As noted above, culture does not determine people's behaviour. Yet it does influence action by offering tools to shape and internalise identities, skills, habits and views on the world that both enable (and restrict) people to build strategies of action and restrict their ability to do so (Swidler 2001: 71–88).[6] Culture affects action in different ways in different situations, however. Swidler (1986: 278–82; 2001: 89–107) indicates that in periods of continuity, which she calls 'settled lives', there is a more 'loose coupling' between culture and action, as people

---

[6] Swidler uses the term 'strategies of action' not in an instrumental way as consciously trying to reach a certain goal, but rather to denote more general, 'larger ways of trying to organize a life' that might allow one to reach several different life goals (1986: 276–7).

naturally know how to act. In such periods, people follow well-established (yet diverse) patterns of action. Culture plays a role by anchoring existing patterns of action and providing both a 'model of' and a 'model for' reality (Geertz 1973). In periods of social change – 'unsettled lives' in Swidler's terminology – culture impacts people's actions more directly. In such periods, actors draw on their cultural repertoires to construe new strategies of action, often in competition with other actors. Central to shaping these new patterns of action are ideologies: explicit and highly organised meaning systems that aspire to offer a unifying answer to new problems (Swidler 1986: 278–9). Ideologies supply assemblages of tools (e.g. world views, rituals, guidelines for action) that teach people how to act in new ways in the world. Especially in situations of conflict with other meaning systems, ideologies offer more coherent cultural packages which structure action in more unified ways. Accordingly, in periods of social transformation, culture influences (new lines of) action more directly, often through (new or transformed) ideologies. Nevertheless, in these cases, too, culture must always be studied in its entanglement with other factors, as it is in concrete contexts that (new) ideologies might become an appealing option and are acted upon.

This approach to culture is useful to further research on Islam and suicide attacks. Perceiving Islamic traditions as part of the cultural repertoires that are available to Muslims avoids binary oppositions between a (decontextualised) Islam and (alleged) secular factors. It allows a more sophisticated analysis of the role of religion, by acknowledging its flexibility, diversity and contested nature, as well as its interrelatedness with other factors. Moreover, by emphasising people's agency rather than viewing them as passive products of culture, this approach enables analysis of how culture is used to shape action, not just in an instrumental way, but also in expressive social practices.

More concretely, the cultural toolkit metaphor raises questions such as: Which tools do the perpetrators of suicide attacks draw from their cultural repertoire to shape and give meaning to their actions? How do they reinterpret and use tools such as particular texts, beliefs, stories and roles in different historical and cultural situations? What does the creation and use of assemblages of tools tell us about the emergence and spread of suicide attacks in specific contexts, and about the diversity in both the instrumental usage of and the social meanings given to the practice? Addressing questions like these will advance our understanding of the role Islam in suicide attacks.

3 Islam and Suicide Attacks

This section will illustrate the insights presented in Section 2 by focusing on different kinds of tools that have frequently been used by suicide bombers and their organisations in varying contexts, such as early Islamic martyr-dom traditions, conceptions of honour, purification and sacrifice, and ritual practices. It will explore the use of these tools by drawing from existing research from the field of religious studies and related fields and disciplines, which has rarely been integrated into terrorism research until now.[7] The section will apply these insights to some cases, and especially the case of al-Qaeda Central (i.e. the group around Bin Laden in Afghanistan and Pakistan) in the 1990s and 2000s.[8]

3.1 Early Islamic Martyrdom Traditions

As noted in the previous section, suicide bombers' frequent references to Islamic martyrdom traditions are often mentioned as one of the prime indicators of the role of religion in suicide attacks. What do these traditions entail and how do suicide bombers and their organisations use these classical texts and beliefs to give meaning to their actions?

The Arabic term for martyr, *shahid* (pl. *shuhada'*), literally means 'witness' (Kohlberg 2010). In the Qur'an the term is primarily used in this sense (e.g. Q. 2:143, 2:282, 22:78, 24:4), although there are also some verses in which it seems to refer to martyrs (e.g. Q. 3:140, 4:69). Yet both meanings of the term are closely related, as martyrs deliver a testimony of their cause through their actions. They draw attention to their belief system

---

[7] This is illustrated by the fact that the studies mentioned in this section are, almost without exception, not included in literature reviews by terrorism scholars such as Crenshaw (2007) and Ward (2018).

[8] For this purpose, this section draws from the author's previous research on al-Qaeda (Nanninga 2014).

and publicly show their readiness to suffer or even die for it, which might add to its credibility. This makes martyrs powerful advertisers of their belief system and community (Cook 2007: 1–2). Accordingly, martyrs are often seen as powerful tools for shaping and strengthening group identity, while setting the norm for honourable behaviour among group members (Weiner and Weiner 1990: 53–8).

The first martyrs of the Muslim community were those who were tortured and killed for their convictions by Muhammad's opponents in Mecca. Yet, in contrast to Judaism and Christianity (e.g. Bowersock 1995), the successes of Muhammad and the first caliphs meant that the scope for martyrdom due to persecution remained limited in the formative period of Sunni Islam. The most important category of martyrs therefore soon became 'battlefield martyrs' (*shuhada al-ma'raka*): the men killed during the military campaigns of Muhammad and his successors (Kohlberg 1997). These deaths, which the Qur'an typically describes as deaths 'in the way of God' (*fi sabil Allah*; e.g. Q.3:169; 9:111), provide the main source for martyrdom traditions among Sunni Muslims. As a result, the *hadith* collections, biographies (*al-sira*) and accounts of Muhammad's raids (*maghazi*) that were composed in the first centuries after Muhammad's death closely connect the concept of martyrdom to the waging of *jihad* (in the sense of armed struggle).

This literature vividly depicts the lives and deaths of the early Islamic battlefield martyrs, as well as their rewards in the afterlife. According to these sources, Muslims who are killed while waging *jihad* enter Paradise immediately after their deaths (see Q. 2:154, 3:169–70; 4:74, 9:20–2, 9:111 and 47:4–6). Their sins are forgiven with the first drop of blood, they are spared the punishment of the grave and they are given delightful rewards, including green gardens, plenty of fruit, heavenly odours, such as the scent of musk, as well as the women of Paradise – the mysterious black-eyed *houri*s (e.g. Q. 44:50–4, 52:18–27; al-Bukhari 1997: 4.56.6, no. 2794, 50–1; 4.60.1, no. 3327, 326–7; Al-Tirmidhi 2007: 5.44.3, no. 3011, 326). Other traditions tell that the souls of martyrs 'live in the bodies of green birds who have their nests in chandeliers hung from the throne of the Almighty. They eat the fruits of Paradise from wherever they like and then nestle in these chandeliers' (Abu Dawud 2008: 3.15.25, no. 2520, 216; Muslim 2007: 5.33.33, no. 1887, 221).

The Islamic legal literature that came into being in the Middle Ages had a more formal tone (Cook 2007: 40). A central concern of Islamic jurists was the definition of what constitutes a martyr. This definition gradually broadened after the early conquests had passed their peak and the number of battlefield martyrs dropped. It started to include, among others, people who died prematurely due to accidents or diseases such as the plague, as well as people who died while engaged in a meritorious act such as pilgrimage or prayer (Kohlberg 1997). Another debate among legal scholars concerned the permissibility of actively seeking martyrdom. Since martyrdom in Sunni Islam has always been closely connected to the battlefield, it has a more active connotation than martyrdom in Judaism and Christianity. Moreover, there exist several traditions about early Muslims who wished for martyrdom (e.g. Q. 3:142–3). Muhammad himself reportedly also expressed this wish: 'By Him in Whose hands my soul is! I would love to be martyred in the way of God and then come back to life and be martyred, and then come back to life again and then get martyred, and then come back to life again and then get martyred' (al-Bukhari 1997: 4.56.7, no. 2979, 52; Muslim 2007: 5.33.28, no. 1876, 209–10). Some of Muhammad's companions are even told to act on their desire. During the Battle of Badr in 624 CE, for example, 'Umayr ibn al-Humam al-Ansari said he longed to be among the residents of Paradise. After Muhammad had assured him that he would definitely be among them, 'Umayr threw away the dates he was eating, advanced towards their Meccan opponents and 'fought them until he was killed' (Muslim 2007: 5.33.41, no. 1901, 234).

Despite traditions like these, Islamic scholars remain divided over the permissibility of seeking martyrdom. Most scholars consider the intention (*niyya*) of the actor decisive in this respect: when an action is carried out for the perpetrator's personal gain it must be condemned, but when it is done for the sake of religion it can be considered martyrdom (Cook 2007: 41–2). Traditions like these would provide useful tools for suicide bombers and their organisations. Yet, rather than simply explaining the behaviour of contemporary believers, these traditions have been reinterpreted and transformed by believers in new contexts. This is illustrated by the cases of Iran, Palestine, 'Abdullah 'Azzam and al-Qaeda.

3.2 Modern Reinterpretations

Iran

Where martyrdom has long remained a subordinate theme in Sunni Islam, Shia Muslims developed an extensive martyrology at an early stage (Günther 1994). Shia martyrdom traditions find their roots in the assassination of Muhammad's cousin and son-in-law 'Ali in 661 CE and, more importantly, the killing of 'Ali's son Husayn by the troops of his Umayyad rival Yazid during the Battle of Karbala in 680. The martyrdom of Husayn on the tenth day (*'ashura*) of the month of Muharram became a central symbol for the 'party of 'Ali' (*Shi'at 'Ali*, hence, Shia), who still remember and re-enact his death each *'ashura*.

The narrative of Husayn's martyrdom has been repeatedly reinterpreted, however. In particular, in the course of the 1960s and 1970s, Iranian ideologues such as Ayatollah Khomeini, 'Ali Shati'ati and Morteza Motahhari provided the tradition with new meanings, which reflected the Iranian political context at that time (Aghaie 2001; Khosrokhavar 2005: 31–48). They compared Husayn's battle against the 'oppressive' rule of Yazid with their opposition against the Shah. Just as Husayn had stepped up against Yazid, they argued, Muslims should rise against the Shah, even if it would result in their death. Moreover, they insisted that Husayn had known in advance that he would lose the battle and be killed, yet continued with his plan. Likewise, Iranians should actively opt for martyrdom in their battle against injustice. 'Every month of the year is Muharram, every day of the month Ashura and every piece of land Karbala', Shari'ati exclaimed during a speech on *'ashura* in 1972 (Rahnema 1998: 315).

Iranian revolutionaries thus transformed Shia conceptions of martyrdom from a predominantly passive tradition of collective remembrance into an objective that should be actively pursued by individual believers. Moreover, they separated martyrdom from the waging of *jihad*, making the former superior to the latter (Aghaie 2001: 168–9; Khosrokhavar 2005: 41–3). Martyrdom was the 'pulsating heart of history', Shari'ati explained (Rahnema 1998: 315). This thought would be translated into practice in the late 1970s, first during the Iranian revolution and later in the war against

Iraq, in which numerous young Iranians were mobilised to defend the revolution against the present-day Yazids. The Karbala tradition provided the model for action that enabled the Iranian revolutionaries to dramatise their political struggles (Kippenberg 1981; Riesebrodt 1998: 137–8).

Palestine

Lebanese ideologues who started to promote 'martyrdom operations' against Israel in the 1980s borrowed the Karbala-inspired martyrdom discourse directly from their Iranian counterparts (Cook 2007: 141). Sunni Muslims, however, lacked such an authoritative model and, accordingly, they had never fostered the activist notion of self-sacrifice that characterised modern Shia reinterpretations of the Karbala narrative. Nevertheless, several Sunni ideologues and activists would devote considerable attention to the topic of martyrdom in the twentieth century. Together with the Lebanese ideologues and organisations, these thinkers would lay the basis for Hamas's cultivation of 'martyrdom operations' in the 1990s.

One of the most prominent thinkers in this respect was Sayyid Qutb, whose writings on *jihad* include significant sections on martyrdom. Moreover, in his attempts to legitimise resistance against the Egyptian regime, Qutb appropriated classical martyrdom traditions. The last part of his *Milestones along the Road* (Qutb 1979), for example, is devoted to the story of the Companions of the Pit (*ashab al-ukhdud*), who had been tortured and killed for their beliefs (Q. 85:1–9; Cook 2008). According to Qutb, the bodies of these companions might have been burned, but they nevertheless gained victory through their self-sacrifice. Qutb's ideas on the victorious nature of martyrdom would be further developed by Muhammad 'Abd al-Salam Farag and the Egyptian group al-Gama'at al-Islamiyya. The latter started debating the option of adopting 'martyrdom operations' in the early 1990s (Cook 2007: 141–2), around the time Hamas executed its first suicide attacks.

Martyrdom has been important in Hamas's discourse since its establishment during the First Intifada, as is witnessed by frequent references to the concept in its 1988 Charter as well as in the leaflets it distributed during the uprising (Maqdisi 1993; Mishal and Aharoni 1994). These documents show that Hamas uses numerous quotations from the Qur'an and *hadith* collections to promote self-sacrifice for the liberation of Palestine. Hamas embraced a notion of martyrdom as propagated by Qutb and his colleagues, yet it offered a distinctly Palestinian version. It not only embedded martyrdom in the Palestinian *jihad*, but it also appropriated Palestinian martyrs as its prime symbols, such as 'Izz al-Din al-Qassam, who had been killed during a revolt against the British in 1936.

Hamas had thus already cultivated a martyrdom tradition by the time it conducted its first suicide attacks in 1994. Accordingly, Hamas embedded these 'martyrdom operations' in the existing martyrdom traditions, rather than presenting them as an entirely new phenomenon. The innovative labels *'amaliyyat istishhadiyya* ('martyrdom-seeking operations') and *istishhadiyyun* ('martyrdom seekers') used to denote the attacks and attackers, respectively, emphasise the active aspect of the action and a degree of intentionality on the part of the actor, rather than the more victim-related associations of the traditional term *shahid* ('martyr'). Yet these terms do connect suicide attacks and their perpetrators to the classical concept of martyrdom (*istishhad*; Whitehead and Abufarha 2008).

In addition to the terms used to denote its innovative operations, Hamas also selectively drew from classical martyrdom narratives to celebrate its suicide bombers among its supporters and in Palestinian society at large. However, it largely abstained from direct engagement in the fierce theological debates about the permissibility of the operations (see Mishal and Sela 2006: 76–7). Rather, Hamas emphasised the tactical advantages of martyrdom operations in its asymmetrical struggle against Israel. Due to the widespread sympathy for the Palestinian struggle in the Muslim world, opposition to Palestinian suicide attacks remained relatively limited (Cook 2007: 153; Kepel 2008: 89–98).

'Abdullah 'Azzam

Hamas opened the door for other Sunni groups to embrace suicide attacks, among which were global jihadists (Moghadam 2008: 104). The latter's conceptions of martyrdom followed a somewhat different trajectory, however. Crucial in this respect was the Palestinian ideologue 'Abdullah 'Azzam, who popularised the 'grand narrative of jihad through martyrdom' during the war against the Soviets in Afghanistan (Kepel 2008: 78; Hatina

2014: 137; Cook 2017: 154–70). In writings and speeches, 'Azzam promoted martyrdom as 'the essence of religion' and the summit of *jihad*, arguing that the blood of martyrs is crucial for success of the *umma*, the restoration of its honour and the building of an Islamic state ('Azzam n.d.). Moreover, 'Azzam celebrated the lives and deaths of martyrs in Afghanistan in reports that typically include lengthy descriptions of their piety and bravery, their heroic deaths and the often miraculous events that happened afterwards (e.g. 'Azzam 1986).

'Azzam drew frequently from classical sources to support his accounts and arguments, typically selecting passages from the Qur'an and *hadith* collections on the status of martyrs and their rewards, as well as on authoritative examples from early Islamic history. These classical traditions are incorporated into accounts that evoke a mysterious or even miraculous sphere. For example, 'Azzam repeatedly associates martyrs with miraculous events (*karamat*), such as martyrs visiting their comrades in dreams and visions after their deaths and their corpses emitting a radiant light or the heavenly scent of musk, even months after they had been buried ('Azzam 1986). Interestingly, 'Azzam openly relied on Sufi thinkers in explaining events like these, despite his general disapproval of these mystical Muslims (Li 2012). 'Azzam's reliance on Sufi writers makes more sense when one realises that miracle stories like these are rather common in the tribal regions across the Afghan-Pakistani border area where 'Azzam lived (e.g. Dalrymple 2005). Accordingly, Darryl Li (2012) argues that beliefs and practices like these provided the Arabs and Afghans with a common vocabulary, enabling local people to identify with the global *jihad*. Yet they also show that early Islamic martyrdom traditions are easily combined with (alleged) heterodox elements and easily blend in local contexts.

Although 'Azzam never promoted martyrdom through self-destruction, his writings have remained highly popular among global jihadists. The respectful yet triumphant tone and the miraculous aura characterising his writings would dominate jihadist martyrologies in the following decades. Martyrs of the Bosnian War, for example, were celebrated in 'Azzam-styled biographies such as the popular audiotape collection *In the Hearts of Green Birds* – a title evidently referring to the earlier mentioned *hadith* describing martyrs as living in the bodies of green birds (Azzam Publications 1997).

But al-Qaeda leaders, and Bin Laden in particular, often struck the same tone and appropriated many elements from 'Azzam's writings (Moghadam 2008: 80–2). Al-Qaeda's martyrologies, however, also included suicide bombers who were, just as in the case of Hamas, embedded in the martyrdom tradition that had developed in previous years.

Al-Qaeda

Al-Qaeda felt the need to address the objections that Islamic scholars raised against suicide attacks in the 1990s and 2000s (see Wiktorowicz 2005; Kepel 2008: 89–105). When one looks at the videos produced by al-Qaeda's media group, al-Sahab, about its suicide attacks and their perpetrators, it becomes evident that al-Qaeda primarily legitimises its attacks by means of strategic and tactical arguments. The *jihad* against the 'occupiers of Muslim lands' is considered obligatory and, given the military superiority of the enemies, suicide attacks are considered the most beneficial way of striking them (e.g. al-Sahab 2002a: 42–7"; 2006b: 6–7"; 2007a: 29–31"). In addition, al-Qaeda repeatedly refutes the argument that suicide attacks equal suicide and are therefore prohibited. 'The opinion of the *fuqaha* [Muslim jurists] regarding this issue is very clear', it claims: when the action is carried out in the interest of Islam, it should be considered martyrdom rather than suicide (al-Sahab 2008a: 20–2"). The biographies of the Prophet's companions also attest to this fact, al-Qaeda indicates. For example, the videos repeatedly refer to the aforementioned Companions of the Pit as well as to 'Umayr plunging himself into the enemies' ranks during the Battle of Badr. According to al-Qaeda, these traditions constitute some of the 'many proofs which clarify and encourage martyrdom operations' (al-Sahab 2002a: 47"; 2007a: 31–2"; 2008a: 35–6"; 2008b: 83–5"). Accordingly, al-Qaeda concludes, the legal evidence that the executors of 'martyrdom operations' should be considered martyrs rather than suicides 'is compelling' (al-Sahab 2002a: 47").

However, although al-Qaeda repeatedly addresses legal questions regarding its suicide operations in its martyr videos, it mostly simply embeds its suicide bombers in the martyrdom tradition that has developed since the 1980s. This is illustrated by the *Winds of Paradise* video series, consisting of a sequence of 'Azzam-styled martyr biographies (al-Sahab 2007b; 2008c). In these videos, men who were killed during battles and airstrikes are presented side by side with suicide bombers, without any notable difference in their portrayals. The videos start with a standardised four-minute introduction that embeds al-Qaeda's martyrs within classical Islamic martyrdom traditions. The introduction starts with computer-generated imagery that relates al-Qaeda's *jihad* to (a romanticised image of) the early Islamic era, showing a tent with a Kalashnikov, an oil lamp, a crackling fire and a Qur'an on a lectern inside. During this computer animation, one of the classic martyrdom verses of the Qur'an is being recited, promising Paradise to those who are killed 'in the way of God' (Q. 9:111). Then the videos feature Bin Laden and 'Azzam, who narrate the tradition about Muhammad expressing his wish to be martyred and speak about the merits of martyrdom, respectively. During 'Azzam's short appearance, the names of the martyrs featured in the video appear in a computer-animated Paradise-like setting, while a *nashid* (hymn) praises martyrs by listing their rewards, which include instant forgiveness for their sins, being spared the punishment of the grave and dwelling in the bellies of green birds in Paradise.

The introduction to the videos thus constantly relates al-Qaeda to classical traditions, expressing the view that those who died in the group's *jihad* are genuine Islamic martyrs. Whether they died due to enemy fire, airstrikes or suicide attacks does not seem very relevant: suicide bombers are included in the videos without any remarks on the controversies surrounding their actions. Accordingly, the video series shows that groups such as al-Qaeda do not only appropriate early Islamic martyrdom traditions to rationalise and legitimise their operations. The opening scene is primarily aimed at presenting a martyrdom mythology that evokes emotions in the audience by means of (possibly appealing) sounds and visuals which together portray al-Qaeda's martyrs as heroic and authentically Islamic fighters. The classical traditions used in the videos add to this imagery by playing on, in Geertz's terms, 'powerful, pervasive and long-lasting moods' among al-Qaeda's sympathisers (1973: 90).

Suicide Bombers as Martyrs

To conclude this section, one should note that the role of early Islamic texts, concepts and stories in the emergence and spread of suicide attacks is a topic of debate among scholars. With regard to jihadists from the West, for example, Gilles Kepel and Olivier Roy have emphasised different aspects. In addition to problems related to integration and the socio-economic position of migrants in the West, Kepel (2002; 2017) underlines the significance of Salafism, and thus of Islamic texts, doctrines and ideologues, in explaining radicalisation and violence. Roy opposes this approach, claiming that it is not the radicalisation of Islam (through Salafism) but rather the Islamisation of radicalism that has produced today's terrorism (Roy 2017: 6). It is disaffected, rebellious youths choosing jihadism as their paradigm for action, he argues with regard to the Islamic State. Accordingly, he emphasises the importance of youth culture, generational revolt and global processes such as the delinking of religion and culture (i.e. the 'deculturation' of Islam, see Roy 2004). These issues lead these youths to piece together a religion without social and cultural embedding, a nihilistic framework that rejects society and is fascinated by death through martyrdom. Roy thus emphasises the social and cultural context of contemporary jihadist 'martyrdom seekers', claiming that 'jihadis do not descend into violence after poring over the sacred texts' (2017: 42).

This section's exploration of the use of early Islamic traditions by (especially) the organisers of suicide attacks does not provide evidence in any direction, as this would require careful empirical analysis of the discourses, beliefs and practices of jihadists in their particular contexts – probably more than both Kepel and Roy have provided up until this point. What this section has shown, however, is that early Islamic traditions have been used in highly diverse and creative ways. Any conclusion in this debate thus needs to be nuanced and specific.

Sunni and Shia groups have selected different parts from their cultural repertoire to authorise and define their martyrs. In both cases, the range of early Islamic sources that they have used is limited, which is not very surprising given the rather scarce support for suicide attacks in the classical sources. The sources they have relied on, however, have been used creatively, in various ways and for varying purposes – not just in an instrumental fashion to rationalise and legitimise suicide attacks for their supporters, potential supporters and larger societal environments (as has been underlined by terrorism scholars), but also to construct a martyrdom mythology that expresses and plays on emotions by portraying martyrs as heroic and authentically Islamic witnesses of their cause.

Moreover, these tools have been employed in innovative ways. Although the classical concepts, texts and stories serve to portray suicide bombers as authentically Islamic martyrs, they have been reinterpreted and transformed in new contexts. On the one hand, these reinterpretations can be perceived as strategic, as is illustrated by the innovative concepts of *'amaliyyat istishhadiyya* and *istishhadiyyun*, as well as by the frequent attempts to relate stories about 'battlefield martyrs', such as 'Umayr, and 'martyrs of faith', such as the Companions of the Pit, to suicide bombers targeting civilians. On the other hand, however, there are more subtle changes in the meanings of the classical traditions, simply because cultural tools gain new meanings when they are employed in new contexts. Accordingly, different types of martyrdom are distinguishable in different contexts. Farhad Khosrokhavar (2005) distinguishes, for instance, between defensive and offensive forms of martyrdom that are dominant in two different kinds of situation: one characterised by problematic or failed nation building (e.g. Iran, Lebanon and Palestine), and the other by globalisation and the attempt to build a new, transnational Muslim community (e.g. al-Qaeda). Yet there are more specific examples illustrating that cultural tools are invested with new meanings once they are employed in new situations. Reinterpretations of the Karbala narrative reflect the Iranian context of the 1960s and 1970s and Azzam's martyr stories were composed by drawing creatively from the different cultural resources at his disposal (including seemingly opposed currents in Islam), as a result of which these stories were embedded in and produced by both the local and transnational contexts of his life and work.

The use of Islamic martyrdom traditions by suicide bombers and their organisations thus underlines that cultural tools are not static and fixed, determining the actions of people in the present day. They are used in complex, dynamic and diverse ways by different agents in different contexts, which can only be understood by relating culture and religion to the historical, political and social situations in which they are being practised. From this perspective, it becomes evident that classical traditions do not produce suicide attacks, even though the perpetrators may imply that this is so. Rather, invoking these authoritative traditions from the past becomes a vehicle for change, enabling agents such as Hezbollah, Hamas and al-Qaeda to legitimise, shape and give meaning to their innovative and contested practices.

3.3 Honour, Purity and Ritualisation

To motivate, shape and give meaning to suicide attacks, the actors involved have used various tools from their cultural repertoire: not just texts, but also socially transmitted practices, roles, values and attitudes. While early Islamic martyrdom traditions have often been mentioned by terrorism researchers, some other themes frequently associated with suicide attacks have gained less attention by terrorism scholars, among them honour, purity and ritualisation.

Honour and Humiliation

Researchers have frequently associated cases of violence with the themes of honour and humiliation (see Blok 2001a; Jones 2008: 121). In cultures with a strongly developed sense of honour – as is the case for large parts of the Muslim world – the violation of honour through public insult and humiliation can result in feelings of shame that, in turn, may fuel violence. Violence can be experienced as a redemption from weakness and disgrace and thus as a restoration of the honour and status of the individual, group or community.

These insights can be illustrated by means of the tribal context of seventh-century Arabia from which Islam emerged. Due to the lack of centralised political power in this period, tribes were central to the social structure. Loyalty to the kinship group and intra-tribal solidarity (*'assabiyya*) were crucial values, which is understandable given the dependence of individuals members on their kinship group for protection. Relatedly, honour was a principal value in upholding the social structure. The status and honour of individuals were strongly connected to their kinship group. Accordingly, when a member of the kinship group was insulted or dishonoured, the reputation of the entire group was affected. The defilement of honour, and thus the appearance of weakness, had to be avenged in order to uphold the reputation of the group and its position in the larger social order. Revenge in the form of violence was often one of the means to do so.

The early Muslims largely adopted these ideas of loyalty, honour and revenge, but primarily applied them to the *umma* rather than to the kinship group. It was now the reputation of the *umma* that had to be protected and, in case of humiliation, avenged (Winter 2002). This was the context in which the notion of *jihad* was developed, and as a result it is closely connected to virtues such as loyalty, honour and revenge in early Islamic sources (Firestone 1999). As noted before, these sources do not directly explain the modern context in which suicide attacks emerged. The honour code of the earliest Muslims has been transformed and redefined over the centuries and cannot be applied directly to the highly diverse cultural contexts in which Islam is practised today. However, honour and shame undeniably still play an important role in many of the regions where suicide attacks have been committed over the last four decades. Moreover, these notions play a significant role in the meanings attributed to this form of violence by the actors involved, as can be illustrated by means of the cases of Afghanistan and al-Qaeda (Nanninga 2014; 2017).

According to anthropologist David B. Edwards, suicide attacks in Afghanistan cannot be explained as merely a practice that was imported from abroad (Edwards 2017: 16). It is crucial to take into account the local cultural context too, which he demonstrates by focusing on the tribal ethos of honour and sacrifice, and the ways in which this has transformed during the wars that have ravaged the country since the 1980s. The Soviet invasion, civil strife and the US occupation disrupted the precarious balance that existed between the state, tribes and Islam, Edwards claims. Traditional ways of upholding social relationships and managing feuds were disrupted, which paved the way for other means to 'resolve' conflicts, among which were suicide attacks.

This can be understood when one realises that upholding a man's reputation (*namus*), which is closely connected to the honour of the family and the nation, is invaluable in the Afghan context. Those who do not succeed in protecting their *namus* are labelled with terms such as *daus* ('cuckold'), *dala* ('lightweight') and *be ghairati* ('cowardly'). Accordingly, men are supposed to prevent assaults on their *namus* and, when their reputation is violated, to restore their honour by taking compensatory actions: erasing the shame by killing the parties involved (Edwards 2017: 143–4). Erasing shame in the traditional way became increasingly difficult during the US occupation, however. The American presence in general and American actions (e.g. house searches) in particular constituted a daily offence to Afghan honour, but it was nearly impossible to respond to such affronts to maintain honour due to the American withdrawal from public space (in armoured cars, compounds, etc.) and from the battlefield (as symbolised by drone attacks). Inaction and thus loss of self-respect and reputation was not an option. In such a context of asymmetrical power relationships, one way of restoring one's honour is to kill oneself alongside (representatives of) those who have defiled one's honour (Edwards 2017: 144–62).

Accordingly, local Afghan values, beliefs and practices associated with humiliation and honour are essential to understand the emergence of a cult of martyrs in Afghanistan since the 1980s. This is particularly noteworthy because this cult provided the local context from which al-Qaeda launched its global campaign of suicide attacks. Moreover, these values, beliefs and practices play a highly significant role in al-Qaeda's discourse on its suicide attacks in the 2000s (see Nanninga 2014: 162–5). The 'globalisation of martyrdom' thus appears to be inherently connected to local situations.

The statements made by al-Qaeda and its suicide bombers are permeated by the idea that the once so glorious *umma* is now humiliated by the enemies of Islam. As one of the 9/11 attackers stated in his farewell message:

> Who reflects upon the state of the *umma* today will find it in a situation not to be envied: extreme weakness and humiliation, tribulation, differences and disregard, and there is no power or might except with God. Our tears cannot even dry from distressing pain ... Spilling of blood, murder of innocents, ravishing of honour and defiling of holy places, yet the whole world watches these butcheries that make apparent the ugliest forms of Zionist-crusader hatred of Islam and its people. (al-Sahab 2003: 13")

Terms such as 'humiliation' (*dhull*), 'weakness' (*wahn*, *da'af*) and 'oppression' (*zulm*) are central to al-Qaeda's discourse, typically in combination with phrases about the honour ('*ird*), dignity (*karama*) and purity (*tahara*) of Muslims and their lands being violated (cf. Khosrokhavar 2009: 75).

In the eyes of al-Qaeda, most Muslims, and especially their leaders, have turned their backs to the suffering of their brothers and sisters. Al-Qaeda and its suicide bombers portray themselves as the ones avenging this disgrace and thus restoring the honour of the *umma*. Bin Laden already said of the *mujahidin* in 1996 that:

> The youths you called cowards are competing among themselves for fighting and killing you [*sic*]. They love death as much as you like life; they inherited honour, generosity, truthfulness, courage and sacrifice from generation to generation. They inherited these characteristics from their ancestors in the pre-Islamic times [*jahiliyya*] and were acknowledged and confirmed in Islam. The Prophet said: 'I was sent to complete and carry out these righteous morals'. (Bin Laden 1996)

In this statement, Bin Laden indirectly quotes one of the famous companions of Muhammad and the commander of the Muslim troops after the Prophet's death, Khalid ibn al-Walid, who once warned the Persian shah in a letter that his Muslim fighters 'love death just as you love life' (al-Tabari 1993: 44). Bin Laden thus implicitly connects al-Qaeda's men to the successful early Islamic warriors. In addition, Bin Laden directly relates his men's 'love of death' to values such as honour and dignity, emphasising the (pre-Islamic) tribal ethos and relating it to self-sacrifice for al-Qaeda's cause.

This relationship between honour and suicide attacks was expressed even more explicitly over the following decades. One of the other 9/11 bombers, for example, stated: 'I take no pleasure in a life of humiliation (*dhull*), and my heart has demanded from me that I live honourably ('*aziza*) in compliance with my Lord's religion, even if that entails leaving loved ones and emigrating'. Thus, he emigrated to take revenge for the disgrace of his community, he continued: 'I have gone out in search of training and means of preparation for *jihad*, so that I might kill Americans and other enemies of Islam and avenge my brothers' blood.' He avenged the dishonouring of his community and 'went out to die with honour', he concludes his statement (al-Sahab 2002a: 50–4").

Al-Qaeda and its suicide bombers present their attacks as the most powerful way to avenge the humiliation of the *umma* in the context of the asymmetrical conflict with its enemies. 'Without a shower of blood, shame is not whipped from the faces', says a poem recited by Bin Laden (al-Sahab 2006a: 10"). Suicide attacks 'eradicate the humiliation that has overcome the lands of Islam' (al-Sahab 2001: 27–8"), al-Qaeda claims in one of its videos, and another states that they 'remove the weakness, feebleness and humiliation that the *umma* is experiencing currently' (al-Sahab 2008d: 3–4"). They bring an end to 'the age of cowardice and weakness' (al-Sahab 2007b: 4"), 'restore the dignity of the *umma*' (al-Sahab 2007a: 45–6") and 'open the door to honour and dignity, a door to victory' (al-Sahab 2002a: 6–7").

These remarks demonstrate that al-Qaeda's suicide attacks were not only an instrumental means to strike its enemies in the most effective way possible. By relating them to conceptions of loyalty, honour and revenge, it becomes apparent that, whatever the direct result of the violence, suicide attacks were conceived as honourable in themselves. Accordingly, they were also expressive practices, conveying perceptions of loyalty, honour, humiliation and retaliation.

These observations add a new dimension to current interpretations of suicide attacks as a means to resist occupation and as a 'weapon of the weak'. These are indeed significant variables to take into account when interpreting the phenomenon, but not merely for the strategic and tactical reasons emphasised by the existing explanations. An additional reason why suicide attacks have often occurred in conflicts against militarily superior 'invaders' might be the fact that, for those who feel humiliated and disgraced, suicide attacks are one of the few options left to those who seek to reclaim agency and restore their honour and reputation and, relatedly, that of their community.

Purification and Sacrifice

Scholars of religion have frequently related violence to the themes of purification and sacrifice. Studies of fundamentalism, for example, indicate that fundamentalist movements and groups are typically characterised by a dichotomised or Manichaean view of the world, meaning that they uphold a strict separation between 'good' and 'evil'. Such a view requires strict boundaries between the own group and the 'polluted' outside world. The perceived purity of the own community needs to be protected and if pollution has penetrated the group, it needs to be removed. This desire for purification can result in violence in order to remove pollution and restore the purity of the community. These ideas, it is argued, are particularly prominent in periods of (perceived) crisis, humiliation and conflict. Fundamentalists often perceive their societies as being in decline from an (imagined) golden era in the past. In order to bring back the glory of the past, the idea goes, society should be purified: polluting elements should be removed and people should return to the pure path of their forefathers (see Riesebrodt 1998: 15–20; Almond, Appleby and Sivan 2003: 23–89; Jones 2008: 135–7).

Religious studies scholars have argued that the violence resulting from such a drive for purification often has a sacrificial nature. Sacrifice, from the Latin *sacrificium*, literally means 'to make holy'. Accordingly, sacrificial violence refers to violence that not only kills and destroys, but also ennobles, transforms and 'makes holy'. Rites of sacrifice, which are found in virtually all religious traditions, thus transform violence into something positive, as it is experienced as removing pollution, cleansing the community and restoring the boundaries between good and evil. In the context of conflict, in which sacrificial rites frequently occur, they may therefore be experienced as providing a sense of control over chaos. They enable members of a community to re-establish boundaries between 'us' and 'them' and thus to achieve greater social cohesion. Moreover, these rites may end periods of violence, as they typically consist of the collective, ritualised killing of a symbolic victim whose death will provoke no reprisals (Girard 1977; Juergensmeyer 2003: 168–74; Jones 2008: 47–55; Edwards 2017: 84–93).

To what extent are these insights relevant to understand suicide attacks? In an influential article, Ivan Strenski (2003) argues that 'human bombers' can indeed be conceived as 'sacrificial gifts' to God and their community. The bombers not only kill themselves, he argues, but, just like sacrifices, they are also, in a sense, 'made holy' through their act. Strenski thus emphasises the social aspect of suicide attacks, as it is the community that accepts or refuses the sacrifice of the bomber. When the sacrifice is accepted, the bombers are 'elevated to lofty moral, and indeed, religious, levels, as sacrificial *victims* themselves or as kinds of holy saints' (Strenski 2003: 8). Their sacredness might also extend to the place of their sacrifice, Strenski argues, which becomes holy by contagion. Accordingly, suicide attacks may be experienced as sanctifying, and thus purifying, the community and its territories.

Despite some criticism of Strenski's ideas (e.g. Asad 2007: 43–4), they are useful when trying to understand the meanings attributed to suicide attacks. This can be illustrated by looking at the cases of Afghanistan and al-Qaeda, which will also enable us to relate the themes of purification and sacrifice to those of humiliation and honour (Nanninga 2014: 165–8).

In his work on the rise of suicide attacks in Afghanistan, Edwards demonstrates that the themes of humiliation, honour, purity and sacrifice are closely related. He argues that tribal, honour-related feuds in Afghanistan were traditionally ended by negotiation and mediation. Central to this process was often an animal sacrifice, which could be seen as a peace offering that provided religious sanctioning to the peace-making process. It can be thought of as a form of meta-communication, Edwards indicates, which allowed people involved in a dispute to switch frames from (honour-related, retaliatory) violence to peace-making without losing face (Edwards 2017: 28–31). Ritual sacrifice could thus put an end to a cycle of reciprocal violence and restore social order. In the context of the wars in Afghanistan since the 1980s, and especially since the US occupation of 2001, however, traditional ways of solving conflicts became increasingly impossible: honour debts could no longer be repaired by either reciprocal violence or animal sacrifice. Moreover, Islamic ideologies, including conceptions of martyrdom, became more important. In this context, the rise of suicide attacks is more easily understood, Edwards argues. As a new form of sacrifice, suicide attacks replaced traditional ways of 'exchanging honour' and enabled the bomber to repay his debt of honour despite the military superiority and physical remoteness of the enemy (Edwards 2017: 211–13).

Although al-Qaeda in the late 1990s and 2000s can evidently not be considered a product of the Afghan context alone, its discourse fits well with Edwards's findings. In line with research on fundamentalist movements, al-Qaeda leaders and suicide bombers typically portray the *umma* as a community in crisis. The glory of the first three generations of Muslims (*al-salaf al-salih*, the 'righteous predecessors') has long vanished and today Muslims are humiliated all across the world, they claim. To restore the successes of the past, Muslims should return to the pure Islam of the first generations. Accordingly, the Muslim community and its lands need to be purified. Suicide bombers are considered to play a prominent role in this respect (e.g. al-Sahab 2001; 2008b).

Al-Qaeda typically presents the martyrdom of its suicide bombers not as a single action, but as part of a lifelong process of self-sacrifice. It is emphasised that these individuals often abandoned their earthly positions and possessions at a young age in order to make the *hijra* ('migration') and join the *jihad*. Moreover, they distanced themselves from earthly life, describing it as a 'fleeting enjoyment' that should be renounced (al-Sahab 2002a: 40"). Often terms are used that recall Sufi mystics practising *zuhd* ('asceticism', 'renunciation'; cf. Kippenberg 2006b: 68–9; Nanninga 2018: 176–7). This process of sacrificing earthly life culminated in their suicide attacks, the videos suggest.

The attacks themselves are often represented in terms related to ritual sacrifice. Bin Laden, for instance, speaks about the 9/11 attacks as an 'offering [*taqdim*] of their lives and necks in the way of God' (al-Sahab 2003: 42") and about the attackers as men 'offering [*qaddamu*] their heads on their palms seeking the pleasure of God' (al-Sahab 2001: 35–6"). Moreover, these ideas of suicide attacks as offerings are explicitly related to the restoration of honour and purity. For example, one of al-Qaeda's videos describes the *mujahidin* as men 'who became certain that the liberation of their sacred places and the lifting of the humiliation [*dhull*] from their *umma* can only be accomplished by sacrificing themselves cheaply in the way of God' (al-Sahab 2006a: 10"). Interestingly, the verb *badala*, which is used in this phrase to denote the sacrifice, implies the notion of 'exchange' (i.e. exchanging one's life for the restoration of sacredness and the undoing of humiliation) – a notion that is also central to the sacrificial logic (see Edwards 2017: 211–12).

In line with these observations, al-Qaeda's martyrs are also often associated with purity. These associations find their roots in early Islamic traditions, according to which martyrs are inherently pure, which is symbolised by their blood. The classical traditions claim that martyrs' sins are forgiven with the first drop of blood they shed. Muhammad therefore ordered that they should be buried in their bloodstained clothes to bear witness to their purity, rather than the clean white sheet in which Muslims are ordinarily buried (e.g. al-Bukhari 1997: 2.23.72–4, no. 1343–6, 245–6; Abu Dawud 2008: no. 3.20.26–7, 3133–9, 575–7).

Al-Qaeda repeatedly calls its martyrs emblems of purity (e.g. al-Sahab 2003: 6"; 2008d: 27"). Moreover, in accordance with the idea of suicide bombers as sacrificial gifts, it is not only the bombers as sacrificial victims themselves who are perceived as being transformed by their death: they also purify their community and its territory by shedding their blood. This becomes evident from al-Qaeda's media releases' frequent connection of the blood of martyrs with terms such as 'washing' and 'cleansing'. In a video about Saudi Arabia, for example, a group of fighters is featured singing about 'protecting the sanctity of Islam' with their blood, after which a voice-over adds: 'Here are the heroes of Islam, who emerged to wash away the disgrace of humility and submissiveness from our foreheads' (al-Sahab 2004: 7"). The youths of Islam are called upon to follow their example in order to 'wash with your blood the humiliation of the *umma*' (al-Sahab 2004: 3"). Statements like these illustrate that the self-sacrifice of the martyrs is considered to remove the humiliation of the Muslim community and restore its honour. Moreover, the blood of suicide bombers 'purified the *umma* from the filth of the treacherous rulers and their followers' (al-Sahab 2002b: 1"), Bin Laden claimed. As in many other cases of violence, the blood of the sacrificial 'victims' is considered to restore the community's purity from pollution by outsiders.

The blood of al-Qaeda's suicide bombers is thus considered to transform both the individuals themselves and their surroundings. The martyr's blood is therefore often associated with fertility and rebirth, expressing hope for the revitalisation of the *umma*. Al-Qaeda leader 'Abu Yahya al-Libi expressed this idea in a statement about one of al-Qaeda's bombers: 'Let his blood and body be a sacrifice [*qurban*] that waters the withered tree of

Islam in the Arabian Peninsula' (al-Sahab 2008a: 17"). Using a Quranic term for ritual sacrifice, *qurban*, al-Libi's statement exemplifies the perception of suicide attacks as sacrifices that purify the community and its territories, thus enabling the dawn of a new era of honour and dignity for the *umma*.

Although al-Qaeda's 'martyrdom seekers' are not made holy through their self-sacrifice in the eyes of their community, the group's discourse definitely demonstrates that it is important to consider the concepts of purity and sacrifice when trying to understand the cultural meanings of the practice. Just like ideas about honour and humiliation, the perpetrators and their organisations appropriate these concepts from their cultural repertoire to shape and give meaning to their actions. In a context of (perceived) humiliation and desecration at the hands of a militarily superior enemy, these tools enable them to regain a sense of dignity, hope and empowerment.

Ritualisation

Like the themes of sacrifice and purity, scholars of religion have frequently related acts of violence to the theme of ritual (see Kitts 2018). It is emphasised that the ritualisation of acts of violence – i.e. providing them with a formal, repetitive and fixed character (Bell 1992: 88–93) – distinguishes them from and privileges them over other, more everyday activities. Moreover, in fusing cognition, emotion and the body, rituals are deemed an effective means of establishing authority and inscribing power on their participants. Providing acts of violence with a ritual structure might therefore facilitate organisations and perpetrators to motivate and legitimise violence among the public. Yet ritualisation is also considered crucial to understanding acts of violence as expressive (rather than utilitarian) practices. Studying a ritualised form of violence provides insights into the meanings it has for the actors involved, as is illustrated by research on violent acts varying from riots and bullfights to public executions and terrorism (e.g. Davis 1975; Blok 2001b; Juergensmeyer 2003). An examination of how perpetrators appropriate rituals and ritual–like practices from their cultural repertoire is therefore important to fully understand cases of violence, including suicide attacks.

The degree of the ritualisation of suicide attacks has varied across time and place. Hamas's suicide attacks in the 1990s, for example, were strongly ritualised (Hassan 2001; Reuter 2004: 87–94; Pedahzur 2005: 170–80). The perpetrators typically spent their last days before their attack according to a standardised pattern which included prayers, recitations, fasting, ritual ablutions and the writing and recording of a last will. These rituals facilitated Hamas's attempts to recruit suicide bombers and increase the social acceptance of the phenomenon (Hafez 2006a: 66–8). In other, more chaotic situations, however, suicide attacks were executed more hastily, lacking a clearly observable standardised pattern. Nevertheless, ritualisation is a significant theme to take into account in seeking to understand the phenomenon, as can be illustrated by a closer look at al-Qaeda's suicide attacks. Although the ritual practices accompanying al-Qaeda's suicide attacks evidently varied on each occasion, it is possible to give a rough structure to the 'ritual process' following Arnold van Gennep's tripartite structure of rites of passage. Van Gennep distinguished three phases in the ritual process that typically characterise a person's transition from one status to another: separation, liminality and reincorporation, signalling removal from the old social position, a transitional stage and the attainment of a new position, respectively (Van Gennep 1960).[9]

During the first phase, al-Qaeda's suicide bombers separated themselves from their old social positions. Often, they physically left their relatives and friends, gave up their roles in society and even left their home countries to join the *jihad* in al-Qaeda's training camps or battlefields in the 1990s and 2000s. Their change in status after their *hijra* ('migration') was symbolised by their new status as *muhajirun* ('migrants'), a classical term traditionally referring to the Muslims who joined Muhammad on his *hijra* from Mecca to Medina in 622. Their abandonment of their old lives was further symbolised by the adoption of a new name: a *nom de guerre* (*kunya*) which typically referred to one of Muhammad's companions or one of the early Islamic warriors (e.g. Fouda 2003: 110–12). Men who were selected to execute a suicide operation were subsequently separated from their peers. From that moment on they again obtained a new status as 'living martyrs' (*al-shahid*

---

[9] For an extended version of this argument, see Nanninga (2016).

al-hayy), which is a classical term used to denote men who were promised the status of martyr during their lives, such as Muhammad's companion Talha ibn Ubaydallah.

During the second phase of the ritual process, the 'living martyrs' entered an ambiguous, liminal position between life and death, which was expressed by several rituals and ritual–like practices that resemble the practices used by Hamas. The significance of these practices can be well illustrated by means of a unique document that belonged to the 9/11 hijackers and was found after the attacks.[10] The four-page, handwritten document contains instructions for the nineteen attackers for the last night and morning before the attack. Yet, rather than paying attention to practical issues, the instructions focus on the spiritual preparation of the bombers (Seidensticker 2006). The 'spiritual manual' guided them through three phases: the last night and morning, the time at the airport and the attack inside the plane. It instructed them to perform all kinds of ritual practices during these phases, including prayers, supplications, Qur'an recitations and ritual ablutions. As a result, all kinds of seemingly mundane actions such as clothing themselves, entering a taxi and passing security checks were ritualised, which, in Hans G. Kippenberg's terms (2011: 179), transformed the attack into an act of worship for its participants.

This is exemplified by the previously discussed theme of purification, which also plays a prominent role in the 'spiritual manual'. Particularly during the night before the attack, the men were to repeatedly perform purification rituals in order to cleanse their hearts and souls, a process that was sealed by the performance of ritual ablution (*wudu*) before leaving the apartment in the morning (Kippenberg 2011: 174–6). Hence, when they re-entered society in the early morning of 11 September, the nineteen men were supposed to be in a state of purity. During the night, they had symbolically removed the last remainders of the world around them and, once they left their apartments, they could be considered beacons of purity in a polluted society. They had symbolically distanced themselves from

---

[10] For a translation of the document, information on its background and further analyses of the ritualised preparations for 9/11, see Kippenberg and Seidensticker (2006); Kitts (2010).

earthly life and simultaneously prepared themselves for their future status as (inherently pure) martyrs.

The ritualisation of the attacks thus made of them acts of worship and purification. Yet it also enabled the attackers to perceive themselves as warriors in the footsteps of the Prophet Muhammad. The actions the hijackers were to perform were constantly related to the practices of the earliest generations of Muslims. The document reads, for example: 'You should clench your teeth, as the early generations [*salaf*] did before they engaged in battle', and 'Tighten your clothes, since this is the way of the pious early generations [*al-salaf al-salih*]. They would tighten their clothes before battle'. Thus, simple actions such as clenching the teeth and dressing properly were related to the authoritative first generations of Muslims. Yet the same was true for less mundane actions, such as the possible killing of passengers in case of resistance. The document says: 'If you slaughter, do not cause discomfort to those you are killing, because this is one of the practices of the Prophet'. Here, the text again compares the 9/11 bombers with Muhammad, meanwhile ritualising the possible killing of passengers by comparing it with the ritual slaughter (*dhabiha*) of an animal.

In relating the actions of the nineteen men to the battles that were fought by Muhammad and his companions, the document expresses the idea that they were re-enacting a 'raid in the way of God [*ghazwa fi sabil Allah*]' (Kippenberg 2006a). This is particularly clear in the last passage of the text. After telling the men that their last words should be either a prayer or the Islamic creed (*shahada*), the document concludes by saying:

> If you see the enemy as strong, remember the confederates [who formed a coalition to fight the Prophet]. They were 10,000. Remember how God gave victory to his faithful servants. God said: '*When the faithful saw the confederates, they said: "This is what God and the Prophet promised, they told the truth."*' (Q. 33:22)

This passage refers to the Battle of the Trench in 627 CE, when 3,000 Muslims are believed to have successfully defended Medina against an overwhelming force of 10,000. Like these Muslims, the hijackers were presented as a minority who will triumph in the end. The perception that they were re-enacting a raid conducted by the Prophet thus served to empower the perpetrators of the 9/11 attacks.

The ambiguous position of 'living martyrs' is thus both expressed in and produced by several rituals and ritual–like activities. It signalled and facilitated the perception that they would be transformed from 'ordinary' believers to martyrs in Paradise, which can be conceived as the third phase of the ritual process of al-Qaeda's suicide bombers. Contrary to the second phase, the third phase is characterised by the *absence* of rituals. According to early Islamic traditions, Muslims who died should be ritually washed and then shrouded in two or three simple pieces of cloth, after which funeral prayers should be offered and the deceased can be buried. In the case of martyrs, however, these rituals are not required (see Kohlberg 2010; Cook 2007: 42–3). As noted before, martyrs should be buried in their bloodstained clothes. Moreover, Muhammad reportedly instructed that funeral prayers not be performed at their graves.[11] This divergent ritual process reflects beliefs about the fate of martyrs, that they do not have to await the Resurrection in their grave but enter Paradise immediately after their death.

With regard to al-Qaeda's suicide bombers, performing funerary rites was evidently not possible in many cases. This was not considered problematic, however. On the contrary, it was perceived as honourable, as becomes clear from the farewell message from one of the 9/11 bombers, who requested God: 'Do not let our bodies be concealed by a grave, nor covered by earth. So that they receive the glad tidings of entering Paradise' (al-Sahab 2002a: 55"). The bomber directly relates the divergent ritual process to beliefs about the fate of martyrs. The destruction of the body has completed the process of separation from earth, and the omission of death rituals underlines the new status of martyr in which the bombers are 'reincorporated' in their community.

To sum up, al-Qaeda thus appropriated various tools to transform its violence into martyrdom operations, including early Islamic concepts, stories and practices and contemporary ritual and ritual–like activities.

---

[11] Whereas this is commonly accepted today, early Islamic traditions actually disagree on this point (e.g. al-Bukhari (1997: 2.23.72, no. 1343, 245; 4.61.25, no. 3596, 481); Abu Dawud (2008: 3.20.26–7, no. 3135/3137, 575–7)).

These tools provided the suicide attacks with a ritual structure that distinguishes them from everyday practices and both expresses and produces the perception that the attackers are transformed from 'ordinary' men to martyrs in Paradise.

Conclusion

The thousands of suicide attacks in the Muslim world since the 1980s require multifaceted explanations. Research has demonstrated convincingly that organisations and individual suicide bombers are driven by different factors, and that both organisations and individual bombers can only be understood in their particular historical, political, social and cultural contexts. Scholars emphasise that organisations using suicide attacks typically make a strategic, calculated choice to adopt this means in their specific situation, which often involves asymmetrical conflict that leads to perceptions of crisis, marginalisation and humiliation. The individuals engaging in suicide attacks are commonly regarded as normal in terms of their psychological, demographic and socio-economic backgrounds. As a result, their (highly diverse) societal environments and social networks have become central to most interpretations of suicide attacks. In sum, the particular political and social circumstances are considered crucial to explaining why organisations and individuals engage in suicide attacks. Given the fact that these circumstances in the regions in which suicide attacks have occurred over the last four decades have been highly diverse, general, all-encompassing explanations for the phenomenon are largely rejected today.

This also implies that the role of Islam is more complex than the predominance of Muslims among the perpetrators of suicide attacks might suggest. Most studies acknowledge the importance of Islamic traditions in shaping and motivating suicide attacks, for example as they facilitate groups to justify their violence, draw recruits and mobilise support. Moreover, Islam is often crucial in the self-understanding of perpetrators from the Muslim world, enabling them to rationalise and give meaning to their violence. However, researchers almost unanimously consider religion to be neither a necessary nor a sufficient condition for suicide attacks. The role of religion can only be understood in combination with political, social and cultural factors: only in particular situations might (specific interpretations of) Islamic traditions fuel suicide attacks. Besides, Islamic traditions are fluid and practised in multiple ways in different contexts. The role of religion is often hard to separate from non-religious factors, so singling out 'religion' or 'Islam' as an explanatory factor is not very helpful.

In line with recent research in the field of religious studies, this Element has suggested that current approaches to the phenomenon of suicide attacks be complemented by one that embeds their organisers and perpetrators in their (highly diverse) cultural contexts – a dimension that has received less attention in the literature. Put more precisely, the suggested approach conceives Islamic traditions as part of the cultural repertoire from which groups and individuals draw 'tools', such as culturally transmitted narratives, beliefs, roles, values and practices, to shape and give meaning to their actions.

Such an approach avoids both a rigid religious-secular divide and a decontextualised, reified perception of Islam that, in the form of a fixed set of texts and beliefs, determines the behaviour of its practitioners. Instead, it emphasises the flexibility of culture (and, thus, religion) and the agency of people, focusing on how people *practise* culture and religion in diverse ways in their particular situations. This not only enables a more nuanced analysis of how Islamic traditions are being used in the highly diverse contexts in which suicide attacks have emerged over the last four decades, it also facilitates analysis of the cultural meanings of that violence for the actors involved. In the current literature, suicide attacks are mainly approached from an instrumental perspective: as an allegedly useful means to accomplish certain ends. However, suicide attacks are also expressive social practices that carry meanings for the participants and 'say' something to the audience witnessing the events. This dimension needs to be taken into account to understand why people engage in or support these seemingly irrational practices. The emergence of al-Qaeda's campaign of suicide attacks out of Afghanistan illustrates this point.

Al-Qaeda's suicide attacks emerged out of a local context that had been ravaged by wars for years. As a result of these ongoing conflicts, traditional Afghan ways of managing feuds and restoring one's honour by means of either retaliatory violence or animal sacrifice had become impossible. Local conceptions of honour, humiliation, revenge and sacrifice changed, which facilitated the rise of a new form of sacrifice through self-destruction. In this context, al-Qaeda's message about the humiliation of the *umma* and the occupation and desecration of its lands found fertile ground. The 'Azzam-inspired ethos of *jihad* through martyrdom appealed to some parts of the local population as well as to Arabs and other *mujahidin* in the region who felt humiliated either directly or by proxy. A more activist interpretation of martyrdom was embraced and propagated by al-Qaeda under the label of 'martyrdom operations', not only as an effective way of striking a militarily superior enemy (as had already been demonstrated in Lebanon and Palestine), but also as the only viable option for restoring the honour and purity of the *umma* and restoring the glory of Islam in the world.

Al-Qaeda's suicide attacks both express and produce these perceptions, as becomes clear from the ways in which al-Qaeda leaders and operatives made creative use of the cultural repertoires available to them to shape and give meaning to their violence. They appropriated various tools, such as culturally transmitted stories (e.g. about Muhammad's raids and 'Umayr's martyrdom), roles (e.g. *muhajir*, 'living martyr' and 'martyr'), values (e.g. loyalty and honour), beliefs (e.g. on purity and Paradise) and practices (e.g. ritual sacrifice, ablutions and slaughter). These tools are flexible and constantly being reinterpreted and transformed in new contexts, as is illustrated by new interpretations of classical Islamic martyrdom traditions in Iran, Palestine and Afghanistan. Along the same lines, al-Qaeda provided new meanings to the tools it assembled, as a result of which they, in concert, transformed self-sacrificial bloodshed into acts of martyrdom. Rather than being mere instrumental actions, al-Qaeda's suicide attacks were also meaningful social practices through which the actors, in Geertzian terms, told a story about themselves – a story that included some of the central themes of their community and ideology. The martyrs acted as empowering 'witnesses' of al-Qaeda's cause who both expressed and produced the cultural context from which the practice emerged. Through their ritualised actions, they signalled the perception that they, as genuine Islamic martyrs, re-enacted Muhammad's raids, thereby restoring the honour and purity of their community and its territories.

In sum, research has gained important insights into the strategic use of suicide attacks by organisations, as well as into the psychological, demographic and social backgrounds of individual perpetrators. Yet more in-depth research on the cultural contexts out of which suicide attacks have emerged is needed to further our understanding of why people engage in or support the phenomenon. This will shed new light on existing interpretations, for example by showing that suicide attacks often occur in asymmetrical conflicts not just because of strategic and tactical reasons, but also because, in such contexts, self-sacrifice might be perceived as the only viable option to restore honour without losing face. In addition, embedding suicide attacks in their cultural contexts offers a more useful perspective on the role of Islam in the thousands of suicide attacks that have targeted the Muslim world over the last four decades. Instead of artificially distinguishing between alleged Islamic and other cultural factors, both can be perceived as part of the cultural repertoire from which people draw to shape and give meaning to their actions. Comparative research on suicide attacks along these lines will extend our understanding of how, why and under which circumstances particular assemblages of narratives, beliefs, roles, values and practices facilitate the perception that killing oneself alongside others is the right thing to do.

Bibliography

Abu Dawud Sulayman bin Ash'ath. 2008. *Sunan Abu Dawud*, transl. Nasiruddin al-Khattab, 5 vols., Riyadh: Maktaba Darussalam, https://islamfuture.wordpress.com/2013/07/08/sunan-abu-dawood-5-vol-set.

Aghaie, Kamran. 2001. The Karbala Narrative: Shī'ī Political Discourse in Modern Iran in the 1960s and 1970s, *Journal for Islamic Studies* 12:2, 151–76.

Alexander, Jeffrey C. 2004. Cultural Pragmatics: Social Performance between Ritual and Strategy, *Sociological Theory* 22:1, 88–105.

Almond, Gabriel A., R. Scott Appleby and Emmanuel Sivan. 2003. *Strong Religion: The Rise of Fundamentalisms around the World*, Chicago: The University of Chicago Press.

Appleby, R. Scott. 2000. *The Ambivalence of the Sacred: Religion, Violence, and Reconciliation*, Lanham: Rowman & Littlefield Publishers, Inc.

Asad, Talal. 1993. *Genealogies of Religion: Discipline and Reasons of Power in Christianity and Islam*, Baltimore: Johns Hopkins University Press.

2003. *Formations of the Secular: Christianity, Islam, Modernity*, Stanford: Stanford University Press.

2007. *On Suicide Bombing*, New York: Columbia University Press.

Atran, Scott. 2003. Genesis of Suicide Terrorism, *Science* 299, 1534–9.

2006. The Moral Logic and Growth of Suicide Terrorism, *Washington Quarterly* 29:2, 127–47.

'Azzam, 'Abdullah. n.d. Martyrs: The Building Blocks of Nations, transl. Azzam Publications, n.p.: Azzam Publications, https://english.religion.info/2002/02/01/document-martyrs-the-building-blocks-of-nations.

1986. *Ayat al-rahman fi jihad al-afghan* [The Signs of the Merciful in the Afghan Jihad], Amman: Maktaba al-Manar, https://archive.org/details/aayat.afghan.g.

Azzam Publications. 1997. *In the Hearts of the Green Birds: the Martyrs of Bosnia*, London: Azzam Publications, https://archive.org/details/In_The_Heart_Of_Green_Birds.

Baumann, Gerd. 1999. *The Multicultural Riddle: Rethinking National, Ethnic and Religious Identities*, New York and London: Routledge.

Bell, Catherine. 1992. *Ritual Theory, Ritual Practice*, Oxford: Oxford University Press.

Bin Laden, Osama. 1996. I'lan al-jihad 'al al-Amrikiyyin al-muhtalin li-Bilad al-Haramayn [Declaration of Jihad against the Americans Occupying the Land of the Two Holy Places], *Al-Quds al-'Arabi*, 23 August, https://ctc.usma.edu/harmony-program/declaration-of-jihad-against-the-americans-occupying-the-land-of-the-two-holiest-sites-original-language–2/.

2002. Full text: Bin Laden's 'Letter to America', 6 October, unknown transl., *Observer*, www.theguardian.com/world/2002/nov/24/theobserver.

Blok, Anton. 2001a. Introduction, in Anton Blok, *Honour and Violence*, Cambridge: Polity Press, 1–13.

2001b. The Meaning of 'Senseless' Violence (1991), in Anton Blok, *Honour and Violence*, Cambridge: Polity Press, 103–14.

Bloom, Mia M. 2004. Palestinian Suicide Bombing: Public Support, Market Share and Outbidding, *Political Science Quarterly* 119:1, 61–88.

2005. *Dying to Kill: The Allure of Suicide Terror*, New York: Columbia University Press.

2006. Dying to Kill: Motivations for Suicide Terrorism, in Ami Pedahzur (ed.), *Root Causes of Suicide Terrorism: The Globalization of Martyrdom*, London: Routledge, 25–53.

2007. Female Suicide Bombers: A Global Trend, *Daedalus* 136:1, 94–102.

Bowersock, G. W. 1995. *Martyrdom and Rome*, Cambridge: Cambridge University Press.

Brunner. Claudia. 2007. Occidentalism Meets the Female Suicide Bomber: A Critical Reflection on Recent Terrorism Debates: A Review Essay, *Signs: Journal of Women in Culture and Society* 32:4, 957–71.

Al-Bukhari, Muhammad ibn Isma'il. 1997. *Sahih al-Bukhari*, transl. Muhammad Muhsin Khan, 9 vols., Riyadh: Maktaba Darussalam, https://islamfuture.wordpress.com/2012/11/25/sahih-al-bukhari-9-vol-set.

Cavanaugh, William T. 2009. *The Myth of Religious Violence: Secular Ideology and the Roots of Modern Conflict*, Oxford: Oxford University Press.

Cook, David. 2005. *Understanding Jihad*, Berkeley: University of California Press.

2007. *Martyrdom in Islam*, Cambridge: Cambridge University Press.

2008. The *Ashāb al-Ukhdūd*: History and *Hadīth* in a Martyrological Sequence, *Jerusalem Studies in Arabic and Islam* 34, 125–48.

2017. Contemporary Martyrdom: Ideology and Material Culture, in Thomas Hegghammer (ed.), *Jihadi Culture: The Art and Social Practices of Militant Islamists*, Cambridge: Cambridge University Press, 128–50.

CPOST (Chicago Project on Security and Threats). 2018. Suicide Attack Database, University of Chicago, https://cpost.uchicago.edu/database.

Crenshaw, Martha. 1998. The Logic of Terrorism: Terrorist Behaviour as a Product of Strategic Choice, in Walter Reich and Walter Laqueur (eds.), *Origins of Terrorism: Psychologies, Ideologies, Theologies, States of Mind*, Baltimore: Woodrow Wilson Center Press, 7–24.

2001. 'Suicide' Terrorism in Comparative Perspective, in *Countering Suicide Terrorism: An International Conference*, Herzlia: International Policy Institute for Counter-Terrorism, 21–29.

2007. Explaining Suicide Terrorism: A Review Essay, *Security Studies* 16:1, 133–62.

Dalrymple, William. 2005. Inside Islam's 'Terror Schools', *New Statesman*, 28 March, www.newstatesman.com/politics/international-politics/ 2014/04/inside-islams-terror-schools.

Davis, Natalie Zemon. 1975. Rites of Violence (1973), in Natalie Zemon Davis, *Society and Culture in Early Modern France*, Stanford: Stanford University Press, 152–87.

Durkheim, Émile. 1897. *Le Suicide: étude de sociologie*, Paris: Félix Alcan.

Edwards, David B. 2017. *Caravan of Martyrs: Sacrifice and Suicide Bombing in Afghanistan*, Oakland: University of California Press.

Eickelman, Dale F., and James Piscatori. 2004. *Muslim Politics*, Princeton: Princeton University Press.

Firestone, Reuven. 1999. *Jihad: The Origin of Holy War in Islam*, Oxford: Oxford University Press.

Fouda, Yosri, and Nick Fielding. 2003. *Masterminds of Terror: The Truth behind the Most Devastating Terrorist Attack the World Has Ever Seen*, New York: Arcade Publishing.

Gambetta, Diego. 2005. Can We Make Sense of Suicide Missions? in Diego Gambetta (ed.), *Making Sense of Suicide Missions*, Oxford: Oxford University Press, 259–300.

Geertz, Clifford. 1973a. Religion as a Cultural System, in Clifford Geertz, *The Interpretations of Cultures*, New York: Basic Books, 87–125.

1973b. Deep Play. Notes on the Balinese Cockfight (1972), in Clifford Geertz, *The Interpretation of Cultures*, New York: Basic Books, 412–53.

Gerges, Fawaz A. 2005. *The Far Enemy: Why Jihad Went Global*, Cambridge: Cambridge University Press.

Gill, Paul. 2013. Tipping Point: The Adoption of Suicide Bombing, *Psicología Política* 46, 77–94.

Ginges, Jeremy, Ian Hansen and Ara Norenzayan. 2009. Religion and Support for Suicide Attacks, *Psychological Science* 20:2, 224–30.

Girard, René. 1977. *Violence and the Sacred* (1972), transl. Patrick Gregory, Baltimore: Johns Hopkins University Press.

Graitl, Lorenz. 2017. Terror as Sacrificial Ritual? A Discussion of (Neo-) Durkheimian Approaches to Suicide Bombing, in James R. Lewis (ed.), *The Cambridge Companion to Religion and Terrorism*, Cambridge: Cambridge University Press, 116–31.

Gunning, Jeroen. 2009. *Hamas in Politics: Democracy, Religion and Violence*, New York: Columbia University Press.

and Richard Jackson. 2011. What's so 'Religious' about 'Religious Terrorism'?, *Critical Studies on Terrorism* 4:3, 369–88.

Günther, Sebastian. 1994. *Maqâtil* Literature in Medieval Islam, *Journal of Arabic Literature* 25:3, 192–212.

Hafez, Mohammed M. 2006a. Dying to Be Martyrs: The Symbolic Dimension of Suicide Terrorism, in Ami Pedahzur (ed.), *Root Causes of Suicide Terrorism: The Globalization of Martyrdom*, London and New York: Routledge, 54–80.

2006b. *Manufacturing Human Bombs: The Making of Palestinian Suicide Bombers*, Washington, DC: United States Institute of Peace.

2006c. Suicide Terrorism in Iraq: A Preliminary Assessment of the Quantitative Data and Documentary Evidence, *Studies in Conflict and Terrorism* 29:6, 591–619.

2007. *Suicide Bombers in Iraq: The Strategy and Ideology of Martyrdom*, Washington, DC: United States Institute of Peace Press.

Hansen, Stig Jarle. 2012. Revenge or Reward? The Case of Somalia's Suicide Bombers, *Journal of Terrorism Research* 1:1, 15–40.

Hassan. Nasra. 2001. An Arsenal of Believers: Talking to the 'Human Bombs', *The New Yorker* 77, 19 November, 36–42.

Hatina, Meir. 2014. *Martyrdom in Modern Islam: Piety, Power, and Politics*, Cambridge: Cambridge University Press.

Henne, Peter S. 2012. The Ancient Fire: Religion and Suicide Terrorism, *Terrorism and Political Violence* 24:1, 38–60.

Hill, Peter. 2005. Kamikaze, 1943–5, in Diego Gambetta (ed.), *Making Sense of Suicide Missions*, Oxford: Oxford University Press, 1–39.

Hoffman, Bruce. 1995. Holy Terror: The Implications of Terrorism Motivated by a Religious Imperative, *Studies in Conflict and Terrorism* 1995:4, 271–84.

   and Gordon H. McCormick. 2004. Terrorism, Signalling, and Suicide Attack, *Studies in Conflict and Terrorism* 27:4, 243–81

   2017. *Inside Terrorism*, 3rd edn., New York: Columbia University Press.

Horgan, John. 2014. *The Psychology of Terrorism*, New York: Routledge.

Jackson, Richard, Lee Jarvis, Jeroen Gunning and Marie Breen-Smith. 2011. *Terrorism: A Critical Introduction*, Houndmills: Palgrave Macmillan.

JMCC (Jerusalem Media and Communication Center). 2002. Poll No. 47, December 2002 – Poll Result on Palestinian Attitudes Towards the Palestinian Situation in General, www.jmcc.org/documentsandmaps .aspx?id=452.

Jones, James W. 2008. *Blood that Cries out from the Earth: The Psychology of Religious Terrorism*, Oxford: Oxford University Press.

Joscelyn, Thomas. 2016. The Islamic State's Prolific 'Martyrdom' Machine, *The Long War Journal: A Project of the Foundation for Defense of Democracies*, www.longwarjournal.org/archives/2016/06/the-isla mic-states-prolific-martyrdom-machine.php.

Juergensmeyer, Mark. 2003. *Terror in the Mind of God: The Global Rise of Religious Violence*, 2nd edn., Berkeley: University of California Press.

Kepel, Gilles. 2002. *Jihad: The Trail of Political Islam*, transl. Anthony F. Roberts, Cambridge: Harvard University Press.

2008. *Beyond Terror and Martyrdom: The Future of the Middle East*, transl. Pascale Ghazaleh, Cambridge: Harvard University Press.

2017. *Terror in France: The Rise of Jihad in the West*, 2nd edn., Princeton: Princeton University Press.

Khosrokhavar, Farhad. 2005. *Suicide Bombers: Allah's New Martyrs*, transl. David Macey, London: Pluto Press.

2009. *Inside Jihadism: Understanding Jihadi Movements Worldwide*, London: Paradigm Publishers.

Kippenberg, Hans G. 1981. Jeder Tag 'Ashura, jedes Grab Karbala: Zur Ritualisierung der Straßenkämpfe im Iran, in Kurt Greussing (ed.), *Religion und Politik im Iran*, Frankfurt am Main: Syndikat, 217–56.

2006a. Defining the Present Situation of Muslims and Re-enacting the Prophet's Ghazwas, in Hans G. Kippenberg and Silman Seidensticker (eds.), *The 9/11 Handbook: Annotated Translation and Interpretation of the Attackers' Spiritual Manual*, London and Oakville: Equinox Publishing, 47–58.

2006b. The Social Matrix of the Attack, in Hans G. Kippenberg and Silman Seidensticker (eds.), *The 9/11 Handbook: Annotated Translation and Interpretation of the Attackers' Spiritual Manual*, London and Oakville: Equinox Publishing Ltd, 59–69.

2011. *Violence as Worship: Religious Wars in the Age of Globalization*, transl. Brian McNeil, Stanford: Stanford University Press.

and Silman Seidensticker (eds.). 2006. *The 9/11 Handbook: Annotated Translation and Interpretation of the Attackers' Spiritual Manual*, London and Oakville: Equinox Publishing Ltd.

Kirby, Aidan. 2007. The London Bombers as 'Self-Starters': A Case Study in Indigenous Radicalization and the Emergence of Autonomous Cliques, *Studies in Conflict and Terrorism* 30:5, 415–28.

Kitts, Margo. 2010. The Last Night: Ritualized Violence and the Last Instructions of 9/11, *Journal of Religion* 90:3, 283–312.

2018. *Elements of Ritual and Violence*, Cambridge: Cambridge University Press.

Kohlberg, E. 1997. *Medieval Muslim Views on Martyrdom*. The Hague: Mededelingen der Koninklijke Nederlandse Academie van Wetenschappen.

2010. Shahīd, in *Encyclopaedia of Islam*, 2nd edn., Leiden: Brill, www.referenceworks.brillonline.com.

Lamont, Michèle. 1992. *Money, Morals, and Manners: The Culture of the French and American Upper-Middle Class*, Chicago: The University of Chicago Press.

and Laurent Thévenot (eds.). 2000. *Rethinking Comparative Cultural Sociology: Repertoires of Evaluation in France and the United States*. Cambridge: Cambridge University Press.

Lewis, Bernard. 2003. *The Assassins: A Radical Islamic Sect*, 3rd edn., New York: Basic Books.

Li, Darryl. 2012. Taking the Place of Martyrs: Afghans and Arabs under the Banner of Islam, *Arab Studies Journal* 20:1, 12–39.

Malory, Nye. 1999. Religion Is Religioning? Anthropology and the Cultural Study of Religion, *Scottish Journal of Religious Studies* 20:2, 193–234.

Maqdsi, Muhammad. 1993. Charter of the Islamic Resistance Movement (Hamas) of Palestine (transl. Muhammad Maqdsi), *Journal of Palestine Studies* 22:4, 122–34.

Marway, Herjeet. 2015. Female Suicide Bombers and Autonomy, in Herjeet Marway and Heather Widdows (eds.), *Women and Violence: The Agency of Victims and Perpetrators*, London: Palgrave Macmillan, 110–28.

Merari, Ariel. 2010. *Driven to Death: Psychological and Social Aspects of Suicide Terrorism*, Oxford: Oxford University Press.

Mishal, Shaul, and Reuven Aharoni. 1994. *Speaking Stones: Communiqués from the Intifada Underground*, New York: Syracuse University Press.

and Avraham Sela. 2006. *The Palestinian Hamas: Vision, Violence, and Coexistence*, 2nd edn., New York: Columbia University Press.

Moghadam, Assaf. 2006a. Suicide Terrorism, Occupation, and the Globalization of Martyrdom: A Critique of Dying to Win, *Studies in Conflict and Terrorism* 29:8, 707–29.

2006b. Defining Suicide Terrorism, in Ami Pedahzur (ed.), *Root Causes of Suicide Terrorism: The Globalization of Martyrdom*, London: Routledge, 13–24.

2008. *The Globalization of Martyrdom: Al Qaeda, Salafi Jihad, and the Diffusion of Suicide Attacks*, Baltimore: Johns Hopkins University Press.

Muslim ibn al-Hajjaj, Abu al-Husayn. 2007. *Sahih Muslim*, transl. Nasiruddin al-Khattab, 7 vols., Riyadh: Maktaba Darussalam, https://islamfuture.wordpress.com/2013/01/03/sahih-muslim-7-vol-set.

Nanninga, Pieter. 2014. *Jihadism and Suicide Attacks: al-Qaeda, al-Sahab and the Meanings of Martyrdom*, PhD thesis University of Groningen.

2016. The Liminality of 'Living Martyrdom': Suicide Bombers' Preparations for Paradise, in Peter Berger and Justin Kroesen (eds.), *Ultimate Ambiguities: Investigating Death and Liminality*, New York and Oxford: Berghahn Books, 78–96.

2017. The Role of Religion in al-Qaeda's Violence, in James R. Lewis (ed.), *The Cambridge Companion to Religion and Terrorism*, Cambridge: Cambridge University Press, 158–71.

2018. Among the Believers Are Men: How the Islamic State Uses Early-Islamic Traditions to Shape its Martyr Biographies, *Numen* 65:2–3, 165–84.

2019. Religion and International Crimes: The Case of the Islamic State, in Alette Smeulers, Maartje Weerdesteijn and Barbora Hola (eds.), *Perpetrators of International Crimes: Theories, Methods and Evidence*, Oxford: Oxford University Press, 192–207.

Norton, August Richard. 2007. *Hezbollah: A Short History*, Princeton: Princeton University Press.

Oliver, Anne Marie, and Paul Steinberg. 2005. *The Road to the Martyrs' Square: A Journey into the World of the Suicide Bomber*, Oxford: Oxford University Press.

Pape, Robert A. 2006. *Dying to Win: The Strategic Logic of Suicide Terrorism*, paperback ed., New York: Random House.
    and James K. Feldman. 2010. *Cutting the Fuse: The Explosion of Global Suicide Terrorism and How to Stop It*, Chicago: The University of Chicago Press.

Pedahzur, Ami. 2005. *Suicide Terrorism*, Cambridge: Polity Press.
    and Arie Perliger. 2006. The Changing Nature of Suicide Attacks: A Social Network Perspective, *Social Forces* 84:4, 1987–2008.

Piazza, James, A. 2008. A Supply-Side View of Suicide Terrorism: A Cross-National Study, *The Journal of Politics* 70:1, 28–39.

Post, Jerrold M. 2007. *The Mind of the Terrorist: The Psychology of Terrorism from the IRA to al-Qaeda*, New York: Palgrave MacMillan.

Qutb, Sayyid. 1979 [1964]. *Ma'alim fi l-tariq* [Milestones along the Road], Beirut and Cairo: Dar al-Shuruq.

Rahnema, Ali. 1998. *An Islamic Utopian: A Political Biography of Ali Shari'ati*, London and New York: I. B. Tauris Publishers.

Reuter, Christoph. 2004. *My Life Is a Weapon*, transl. Helena Ragg-Kirkby, Princeton: Princeton University Press.

Riesebrodt, Martin. 1998. *Pious Passion: The Emergence of Modern Fundamentalism in the United States and Iran*, transl. Don Renau, Berkeley: University of California Press.

Roberts, Michael. 2005. Tamil Tiger 'Martyrs': Regenerating Divine Potency?, *Studies in Conflict and Terrorism* 28:6, 493–514.

Rosenthal, F. 2010. Intihār, in *Encyclopaedia of Islam*, 2nd edn., Leiden: Brill, www.referenceworks.brillonline.com.

Roy, Olivier. 2004. *Globalised Islam: The Search for a New Ummah*, London: Hurst.

    2017. *Jihad and Death: The Global Appeal of Islamic State*, transl. Cynthia Schoch,Oxford: Oxford University Press.

Sageman, Marc. 2004. *Understanding Terror Networks*. Philadelphia: University of Pennsylvania Press.

    2006. Islam and Al Qaeda, in Ami Pedahzur (ed.), *Root Causes of Suicide Terrorism: The Globalization of Martyrdom*, London: Routledge, 122–31.

    2008. *Leaderless Jihad: Terror Networks in the Twenty-First Century*, Philadelphia: University of Pennsylvania Press.

Al-Sahab Foundation for Media Production. 2001. *Tadmir al-mudammira al-amrikiyya Kul 2* [The Destruction of the American Destroyer [USS] *Cole* 2], https://archive.org/details/stateoftheummah2.

    2002a. *Wasaya abtal ghazawat Niw Yurk wa-Washintun: Ahmad al-Haznawi* [The Wills of the Heroes of the Raids on New York and Washington: Ahmad al-Haznawi], https://archive.org/details/hznwiwill.

    2002b. The Nineteen Martyrs: 'Abd al-'Aziz al-'Umari, https://archive.org/details/wasiyat-shaheed-alumari.

    2003. American Hell in Afghanistan and Iraq: Sa'id al-Ghamdi, https://archive.org/details/911-will-saeed-al-ghamdi.

    2004. *Badr al-Riyadh 2* [The Full Moon of Riyadh], https://archive.org/details/moon_BR/badr2_wmv.wmv.

2006a. *Al-'ilm lil-'amal: ghazwa Manhatan 1* [Knowledge Is for Acting Upon: The Manhattan Raid 1], https://archive.org/details/GhazwatManhattan1.

2006b. *Al-'ilm lil-'amal: ghazwa Manhatan 2* [Knowledge Is for Acting Upon: The Manhattan Raid 2], https://archive.org/details/GhazwatManhattan2.

2007a. *Wasaya abtal ghazawat Niw Yurk wa-Washintun: Abu Mus'ab Walid al-Shehri* [The Wills of the Martyrs of the Raids on New York and Washington: Abu Mus'ab Walid al-Shehri], https://archive.org/details/Abu-Musab-Walid-al-Shehri-Will.

2007b. *Rih al-janna 1* [Winds of Paradise 1], https://archive.org/details/windsofparadise1_english.

2008a. *Al-qawl qawl al-sawarim: ghazwa al-mu'adhin Abu Gharib al-Makki* [The Word Is the Word of the Swords: The Raid of the Muezzin Abu Gharib al-Makki], https://archive.org/details/AsSahab-TheWordIsTheWordOfTheSwords1.

2008b. *Hisad 7 sanawat min al-hurub al-salibiyya* [The Results of Seven Years of the Crusades], https://archive.org/details/Results.

2008c. *Rih al-janna 2* [Winds of Paradise: 2], https://archive.org/details/windsofparadise2_AMEF.

2008d, *Jihad wa-istishhad: al-qa'id Abu al-Hasan* [*Jihad* and Martyrdom: Commander Abu al-Hasan], https://archive.org/details/assahab_20080708_hi.

Schalk, Peter. 1997. Resistance and Martyrdom in the Process of State Formation of Tamil Eelam, in Joyce Pettigrew (ed.), *Martyrdom and Political Resistance: Essays from Asia and Europe*, Amsterdam: VU University Press, 61–84.

2017. The LTTE: A Nonreligious, Political, Martial Movement for Establishing the Right of Self-Determination of Īḻattamiḻs, in James

R. Lewis (ed.), *The Cambridge Companion to Religion and Terrorism*, Cambridge: Cambridge University Press, 146–57.

Schuurman, Bart, et al. 2018. End of the Lone Wolf: The Typology That Should Not Have Been, *Studies in Conflict and Terrorism* 42:8, 771–8.

Schweitzer, Yoram. 2000. Suicide Terrorism: Development and Main Characteristics. A lecture presented in the International Conference on Countering Suicide Terrorism at ICT, Herzeliya, Israel on 21 February 2000, www.ict.org.il/Article.aspx?ID=779#gsc.tab=0.

  2006. Al-Qaeda and the Global Epidemic of Suicide Attacks, in Ami Pedahzur (ed.), *Root Causes of Suicide Terrorism: The Globalization of Martyrdom*, London: Routledge, 132–51.

Sedgwick, Mark. 2004. Al-Qaeda and the Nature of Religious Terrorism, *Terrorism and Political Violence* 16:4, 795–814.

Seidensticker, Tilman. 2006. The Instructions Given in the *Spiritual Manual* and their Particular Interpretation of Islam, in Hans G. Kippenberg and Silman Seidensticker (eds.), *The 9/11 Handbook: Annotated Translation and Interpretation of the Attackers' Spiritual Manual*, London and Oakville: Equinox Publishing Ltd, 19–28.

Silke, Andrew. 1998. Cheshire-Cat Logic: The Recurring Theme of Terrorist Abnormality in Psychological Research, *Psychology, Crime & Law* 4:1, 51–69.

  2008. Research on Terrorism: A Review of the Impact of 9/11 and the Global War on Terrorism, in Hsinchun Chen et al. (eds.), *Terrorism Informatics: Knowledge Management and Data Mining for Homeland Security*, New York: Springer, 27–50.

Singh, Rashmi. 2011. *Hamas and Suicide Terrorism: Multi-Causal and Multi-Level Approaches*, New York: Routledge.

Speckhard, Anne. 2008. The Emergence of Female Suicide Terrorists, *Studies in Conflict and Terrorism* 31:11, 995–1023.

and Khapta Ahkmedova. 2006. The Making of a Martyr: Chechen Suicide Terrorism, *Studies in Conflict and Terrorism* 29:5, 429–92.

START (National Consortium for the Study of Terrorism and Responses to Terrorism). 2018. Global Terrorism Database, www.start.umd.edu/gtd.

Stern, Jessica. 2003. *Terror in the Name of God: Why Religious Militants Kill.* New York: Harper Collins.

Strenski, Ivan. 2003. Sacrifice, Gift and the Social Logic of Muslim 'Human Bombers', *Terrorism and Political Violence* 15:3, 1–34.

Swidler, Ann. 1986. Culture in Action: Symbols and Strategies, *American Sociological Review* 51:2, 273–86.

2001. *Talk of Love: How Culture Matters*, Chicago and London: The University of Chicago Press.

Al-Tabari, Muhammad ibn Jarir. 1993. *The History of al-Ṭabarī Vol. XI: The Challenge to the Empires*, transl. Khalid Yahya Blankinship, New York: State University of New York Press.

Al-Tirmidhi, Abu 'Isa Muhammad ibn 'Isa. 2007. *Jami' al-Tirmidhi*, transl. Abu Khaliyl, 6 vols., Riyadh: Maktaba Darussalam, https://islamfuture.wordpress.com/2013/06/22/jami-at-tirmidhi-6-vol-set.

Turner, Kathleen. 2016. The Rise of Female Suicide Bombers, *Counter Terrorist Trends and Analyses* 8:3, 15–19.

Van Gennep, Arnold. 1960. *The Rites of Passage*, transl. Monika B. Vizedom and Gabrielle L. Caffee, London: Routledge & Kegan Paul.

Victor, Barbara. 2003. *Army of Roses: Into the World of Palestinian Women Suicide Bombers*, Emmaus: Rodale.

Victoroff, Jeff. 2005. The Mind of the Terrorist: A Review and Critique of Psychological Approaches, *Journal of Conflict Resolution* 49:1, 3–42.

Ward, Veronica. 2018. What Do We Know about Suicide Bombing? Review and Analysis, *Politics and the Life Sciences* 37:1, 88–112.

Weinberg, Leonard. 2006. Suicide Terrorism for Secular Causes, in Ami Pedahzur (ed.), *Root Causes of Suicide Terrorism: The Globalization of Martyrdom*, London: Routledge, 108–21.

Weiner, Eugene, and Anita Weiner. 1990. *The Martyr's Conviction: A Sociological Analysis*, Atlanta: Scholars Press.

Whitehead, Neil L., and Nasser Abufarha. 2008. Suicide, Violence, and Cultural Conceptions of Martyrdom in Palestine, *Social Research* 75:2, 395–416.

Wiktorowicz, Quintan. 2005. A Genealogy of Radical Islam, *Studies in Conflict and Terrorism* 28:2, 75–97.

Wilayat Ninawa Media Office. 2017. *Lanahdiyannahum subulana* [We will Surely Guide Them to Our Ways], https://jihadology.net/2017/05/17/new-video-message-from-the-islamic-state-we-will-surely-guide-them-to-our-ways-wilayat-ninawa.

Winter, Charlie. 2017. War by Suicide: A Statistical Analysis of the Islamic State's Martyrdom Industry, The Hague: International Centre for Counter-Terrorism, https://icct.nl/wp-content/uploads/2017/02/ICCT-Winter-War-by-Suicide-Feb2017.pdf.

Winter, Timothy. 2002. Honor, in *Encyclopaedia of the Qur'an*, Leiden: Brill, 2.447–8.

World Islamic Front for Jihad against the Jews and Crusaders. 1998. *Bayan al-Jabha al-Islamiyya al-'Alamiyya li-jihad al-yuhud wa-l-salibiyyin* [Statement of the World Islamic Front for Jihad against Jews and Crusaders], *Al-Quds al-'Arabi*, 23 February, http://plancksconstant.org/blog/2006/02/fatw2.htm.

Al-Zawahiri, Ayman. 2001. *Fursan tahta rayat al-nabi* [Knights under the Banner of the Prophet], n.p.: Minbar al-tawhid wa-l-jihad, https://azelin.files.wordpress.com/2010/11/ayman-al-zawahiri-knights-under-the-prophets-banner-first-edition.pdf.

Cambridge Elements

Religion and Violence

James R. Lewis
University of Tromsø

James R. Lewis is Professor of Religious Studies at the
University of Tromsø, Norway and the author and editor of
a number of volumes, including *The Cambridge Companion to
Religion and Terrorism*.

Margo Kitts
Hawai'i Pacific University

Margo Kitts edits the *Journal of Religion and Violence* and is
Professor and Coordinator of Religious Studies and East-West
Classical Studies at Hawai'i Pacific University in Honolulu.

About the Series

Violence motivated by religious beliefs has become all too common
in the years since the 9/11 attacks. Not surprisingly, interest in the
topic of religion and violence has grown substantially since then.
This Elements series on Religion and Violence addresses this new,
frontier topic in a series of ca. fifty individual Elements. Collectively,
the volumes will examine a range of topics, including violence in
major world religious traditions, theories of religion and violence,
holy war, witch hunting, and human sacrifice, among others.

Cambridge Elements

Religion and Violence